QP
86
.H48

Hershey, Daniel.

Lifespan and
factors affecting
it

145835

LIFESPAN—AND FACTORS AFFECTING IT

←—LIFESPAN—→

AND FACTORS
AFFECTING IT

⌐AGING THEORIES IN GERONTOLOGY⌐

By

DANIEL HERSHEY, Ph.D.
Professor of Chemical Engineering
University of Cincinnati
Cincinnati, Ohio

CHARLES C THOMAS • PUBLISHER
Springfield • Illinois • U.S.A.

Published and Distributed Throughout the World by
CHARLES C THOMAS · PUBLISHER
Bannerstone House
301-327 East Lawrence Avenue, Springfield, Illinois, U.S.A.

© *1974, by* CHARLES C THOMAS · PUBLISHER
ISBN 0-398-03041-3
Library of Congress Catalog Card Number: 73-16371

*With THOMAS BOOKS careful attention is given to all details of
manufacturing and design. It is the Publisher's desire to present books that are
satisfactory as to their physical qualities and artistic possibilities and
appropriate for their particular use. THOMAS BOOKS will be true to those
laws of quality that assure a good name and good will.*

Printed in the United States of America
I - 1

Library of Congress Cataloging in Publication Data

Hershey, Daniel.
    Lifespan—and factors affecting it.

    Bibliography: p.
    1. Aging. I. Title. [DNLM: 1. Aging.
2. Longevity. WT104 H572L 1974]
QP86.H48   612.6'7   73-16371
ISBN 0-398-03041-3

To Barbara, Michael and Andrea, who keep me young.

To Edna Penn and Gerri Denterlein, who with patience and skill were able to translate my handwritten scribbling into a tangible, typed manuscript.

PREFACE

MUCH HAS BEEN WRITTEN on aging; both scientific and social aspects have been covered. The data are there for those who can avail themselves of a good library. But the papers in the journals and the books, useful though they are, do not provide a focused look at the theories of aging and derivative ideas. So I gathered my books and papers, extracted the essences, and organized the information so that in *Lifespan — and Factors Affecting It* the reader may have a succinct statement of what happens when we age.

I have taught a two-quarter sequence to university graduate and undergraduate students, nurses, engineers and others interested in gerontology using the material in the book. The comments from the classes were gratifying and suggested that this material ought to be published. But I am aiming for a broader readership than only those technically proficient in the field. The general public, the so-called layman, has a vested interest in aging and should know more about the process. Hopefully *Lifespan — and Factors Affecting It* will help fill a few gaps in the body of knowledge available to the public. In an attempt to avoid the trauma that is induced when one meets strange terminology, I have provided a glossary at the end so that the new words may be quickly translated and the reader can get on with the material.

ACKNOWLEDGMENT

WHO WILL NOT DIE? WHO HAS NOT DIED?

L IFE IS A CUMULATIVE HISTORY of events, governed largely by the laws of probability. To the extent that we can alter the odds, I am grateful to the University of Cincinnati for providing the proper milieu for creative writing. For a chemical engineering professor to become involved in geronotology, as I have, is unusual; to find the opportunity to delve into the aging process and teach courses on that subject and help organize a Gerontology Council is a tribute to the fertile, beneficent and free environment of the University. It is a testimonial also to the university tenure system which provides the security the professor requires in order to search for new frontiers.

D. H.

INTRODUCTION

W E BEGIN BY ASKING whether it is true that every living thing must die eventually. The advancing decrepitude with age is unfolded in *Lifespan — and Factors Affecting It* along with the melancholy story of the bodily functions which diminish. Loss of strength, speed and flexibility are lost for the old, as well as a suffering of weakened eyes and glands. With despair we read on about the various theories of aging which are most in favor today.

And then it dawns upon us that if the theories are correct, if they could only give us a hint as to what is really involved in the aging process, we could perhaps use this knowledge towards an attack on the debilitating effects of age. Stopping the aging process is probably impossible, reversing it too seems unreasonable, but could we slow it down? If free radicals are at fault, then we will find a way to neutralize them. If mutations and an impaired immunologic system are the root causes of our destruction, then some drugs can encumber the immune reaction and alter the rate of destruction. If old, cross-linked collagen stiffens us and impairs the permeability of our membranes, slowing our living processes, then we can find a way of removing this old stuff and laying down new collagen.

But if we age and die because of the depletion of some inborn quantity of energy, then we need to find a way of unwinding the life clock more slowly. We need to find a way of decreasing the rate of living, improving the efficiency of living. And we can also account for the wear and tear of living, the diseases, the mental stresses, the breathless running for trains and buses, and the myriad of other heart-stressing, dizzying activities which exhaust our bodies and minds.

While pondering all of this, can we also invent a better measure of age, based not on years but on some physiologic parameter? How old are you? How old are your lungs? How old are your eyes, your heart, your skin or your glands? Some are old at twenty, others are young at fifty; we know not why. Measure my basal metabolism and tell me how old I am?

I wrote this book to pose many questions and suggest answers to some of them. I accept the fact that I will probably die, eventually, but I do not stand helpless. We understand enough about the aging process to be able to suggest directions for research which ought to be fruitful, if only we are able to devote enough time and money to the cause. So let us begin.

Cincinnati, Ohio

DANIEL HERSHEY

CONTENTS

Preface vii

Acknowledgment ix

Introduction xi

PART I - MUST WE DIE? 3

    Chapter 1 - FACTORS AFFECTING LIFESPAN 5

    Chapter 2 - LOSS OF BODILY FUNCTIONS 28

    Chapter 3 - AGING ON THE CELLULAR LEVEL 46

    Chapter 4 - DEATH AND DISEASE - SUMMING UP 66

PART II - WHY WE DIE 72

    Chapter 5 - AGING THEORIES IN GENERAL 73

    Chapter 6 - SOME FAVORED MICROSCOPIC
              THEORIES OF AGING 81

    Chapter 7 - SOME FAVORED MACROSCOPIC
              THEORIES OF AGING 113

    Chapter 8 - BODY TEMPERATURE, BASAL
              METABOLISM AND AGING 123

    Chapter 9 - SUMMING UP 140

Glossary 141

References 153

Index 157

LIFESPAN—AND FACTORS AFFECTING IT

PART I

MUST WE DIE?

ARE YOU SURE THAT EVENTUALLY YOU WILL DIE? IS THERE ANY- ONE IN THE HISTORY OF OUR WORLD WHO HAS NOT DIED?

THE QUESTIONS SEEM SILLY, FOR WE KNOW THAT SOONER OR LATER EVERY LIVING THING DIES. BUT WHEN YOU BEGIN TO ANALYZE THE STATISTICS OF LIVING AND DYING, YOU REALIZE THAT THE CHANCES OF DYING ARE NOT THE SAME FOR EVERYONE. A NEWBORN BABY, A YOUNG CHILD, A MATURE ADULT, AN OLD MAN: ALL DIFFER IN THEIR CHANCES OF DYING.

CHAPTER 1

FACTORS AFFECTING LIFESPAN

SURVIVAL CURVES

IF WE WERE REALLY CLEVER and somehow managed to discover how to stay physiologically young, it is estimated that we would live to a ripe old age of 800 years. But we are not yet so smart and must be content in living on the average to only 67 years, although women live to about 70 years of age. Though medical science has steadily progressed, little has been uncovered about the ultimate lifespan and how to extend it. Thus a man of sixty has a life expectancy which is greater than a man of sixty had in 1789, but the difference is only about two years (43).

A typical survival curve for humans looks something like Figure 1, where we see that during the very early, tenuous years of infancy, the rate of dying is high. During childhood (ten to

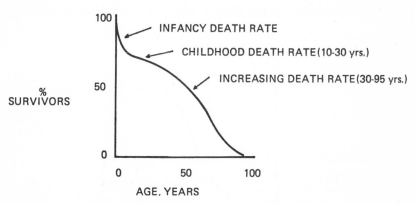

Figure 1.   Typical survival curve for humans (from Strehler [42], p. 89).

30 years) this dying rate is considerably slowed; and then thereafter (30 to 95 years) we die more quickly, with the death rate gradually increasing. The probability of a grown person's

dying doubles each eight years of life. As we approach old age, our chances of dying are obviously quite high. Figure 2 shows another way of looking at survival. Most people seem to die around age 70, but for those who die early, age 40 seems to be the most common for death.

For wolves, that last survivor is gone at about 15 years; for the wild goat all are gone at 23 years; a thoroughbred mare lives longer, lasting till 30 years of age (22). Survival curves seem to look the same, no matter what specie we are considering, even for rats, cockroaches and automobiles (22).

If it were possible to protect living things from all possibilities of unnatural death and provide for complete nutrition and a controlled environment, then, ideally, the survival curve would be similar to that obtained for rotifers, which is shown in Figure 3. These rotifers live to the fullest extent of their biological makeup and reach senescense at around 30 days. At this age they lose their vitality or ability to survive and die off quickly as a group. These rotifers are bred to be genetically similar, with uniform characteristics and potential. Thus their uniform demise is not what might be expected in humans.

We know a dog does not live as long as a human; we know an elephant can live longer than a rabbit. So as we ask questions

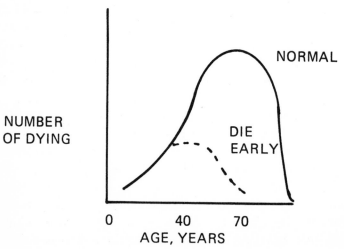

Figure 2.　Numbers dying with age for humans (from Kohn [33], p. 109).

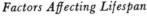

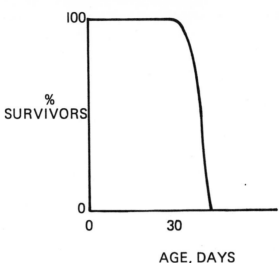

AGE, DAYS

Figure 3. Survival curve for rotifers under ideal, controlled conditions (from Birren [40], p. 132).

about how long we can expect to live, we need to ask additional questions pertaining as to how long one specie will live when compared to another specie. And we must discuss the expected lifespan for those who lead "normal" lives as compared to those who suffer premature deaths due to accidents. Obviously the animals in the wild are more vulnerable to early death. So there are many survival curves, for each specie, all with more or less the same shape, but terminating at different age levels. For example, laboratory mice die off as shown in Figure 4, where we see that the lifespan is on the order of 600 to 900 days. Few deaths occur early in life for the healthy mice reared very carefully in captivity, and so the death rate is very low. Then as the mice reach maturity and old age (about 500 days) they begin to die off more quickly. At 900 days almost no survivors remain. The other curve in Figure 4 shows the survival curve for mice who suffer from leukemia. Where previously we saw that the healthy mice experienced few deaths until they achieved an age of 500 days, the leukemic mice could only expect a similar period of only 100 days. Then their death rate increases sharply, and at age 600 days they are all gone.

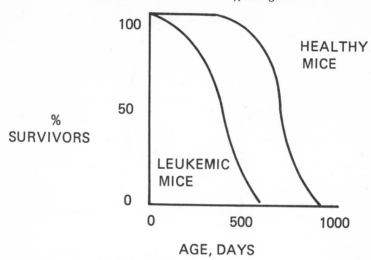

Figure 4. Survival curves for healthy and leukemic mice (from Kohn [33], p. 108).

LIFESPAN OF ANIMALS AND TREES AND THINGS

Determining lifespans of animals is difficult for some very obvious reasons. Certainly there will be differences between those animals that are found in their natural habitat as compared to those in captivity. Questions can be raised about the comparability of life in a zoo as compared to the wild. Diets vary, enemies are different, mating habits and selection of mates are less comparable. Nevertheless some fairly authentic data have been collected as can be seen in Tables I, II and III.

TABLE I
LIFESPAN OF SOME MAMMALS, BIRDS, REPTILES, AMPHIBIANS, FISH AND INVERTEBRATES*

max —maximum on record, years
av   —average, years
c   —in captivity
w   —wild

Mammals

Indian elephant, max. 77, av. 24c
Horse, max. 62, av. 30 small, 20 large
African elephant, max. 57, av.40c
Donkey (ass), max. 50, av. 40

Hippopotamus, max. 49, av. 40c
Indian rhinoceros, max. 45, av. 40c
Chimpanzee, max. 39, av. 15c
Zebra, max. 38, av. 22c

Gorilla, max. 36, av. 26c
Blue whale, max. 36, av. 18w
Lion, max. 35, av. 15c, 10w
Dog, max. 34 spaniel, av. 13 large, 17 small
Capuchin monkey, max. 31, av. 9c
Grizzly bear, max. 31, av. 20c, 25w
Dolphin, max. 30, av. 25w
Shorthorn cattle, max. 30, av. 20
Sperm whale, max. 30, av. 24w

Rhesus monkey, max. 29, av. 15c
Giraffe, max. 28, av. 14c
Pig, max. 27, av. 16
House cat, max. 27, av. 15
Dogheaded baboon, max. 25, av. 11c
Zebu (Indian) cattle, max. 25, av. 11
Moose, max. 25, av. 15w
Fur seal, max. 25, av. 20w
Hyena, max. 24, av. 12c
Little brown bat, max. 23, av. 13w
Sea otter, max. 23, av. 13w
Wapiti (elk), max. 22, av. 14c
American bison, max. 22, av. 10c
Brown bear, max. 22, av. 14c

Fish
Sturgeon, max. 152w, av. 46
Halibut, max. 70
Eel, max. 55c, 15w
Carp (goldfish), max. 50w, 15c
Pacific salmon, max. 41w, av. 12w
Striped bass, max. 20w
Cod, max. 16w

Invertebrates
Sea anemone *Cereus,* max. 90c
Freshwater mussel, max. 80w
Queen termite *Nasuititermes,* max. 60w
Atlantic lobster, max. 50w
Beef tapeworm, max. 35
European crayfish, max. 30c
Blood fluke, max. 28
Sea scallop, max. 22w
American tarantula, max. 20c
Periwinkle, max. 20c, 5w
Queen ant *Lasius,* max. 19c
17-year cicada, 17w

Domestic sheep, max. 20, av. 15 small breeds, 10 large
Tiger, max. 20, av. 11c
Sea lion, max. 20, av. 13c
Big brown bat, max. 18

Gray wolf, max. 16, av. 9c
Mountain lion, max. 16, av. 6w
Pronghorn antelope, max. 15, av. 8c
White-tailed deer, max. 15, av. 8c
Fox squirrel, max. 15, av. 9w
Marmot, max. 14, av. 7w
Raccoon, max. 14, av. 4w
Lynx, max. 12, av. 6c
Dingo, max. 12, av. 4c
Prairie dog, max. 11, av. 8
Deer mouse, max. 8, av. 4c
Cottontail rabbit, max. 8, av. 2w
Opossum, max. 7, av. 3w
Guinea pig, max. 7, av. 2c
Flying squirrel, max. 6, av. 5c
Black rat, max. 4, av. 2w
White (laboratory) rat, max. 4, av. 3c
House mouse, max. 3, av. 15c
Shrew, max. 2, av. 1c, 1w

Sunfish (pumpkinseed), max. 13
Perch, max. 12, av. 10w
Herring, max. 12w
Rainbow trout, max. 9w, 4c
Black bass, max. 8w
Sea lamprey, max. 7w
Sea horse, max. 6c, 2w
Guppy, max. 5c

Mediterranean octopus, max. 12c
Hookworm *Necator,* max. 12
Commercial oyster, max. 12w
Razor clam, max. 12w
Earthworm *Allolobophora,* max. 10c
Large scarabaeid beetles, max. 10
Sea urchin, max. 8w
Queen honeybee, max. 7
Silverfish, max. 7w
Edible snail, max. 7c
House spider (female), max. 7c
Planarian flatworm, max. 7c
Giant snail *Achatina,* max. 6w

Sowbug *Porcellio,* max. 5c
Acorn barnacle, max. 5w
Slug *Limax,* max. 5c

Squid *Loligo,* max. 4w
Chesapeake Bay blue crab, max. 3w
Bay scallop, max. 2w

Birds

Turkey vulture, max. 118w
Mute swan, max. 102c, av. 68c
Sulfur-crested cockatoo, max. 85c
African gray parrot, max. 73c
American crow, max. 69c
White pelican, max. 52w, av. 12w
Ostrich, max. 50c
Domestic duck, max. 47
Bald eagle, max. 44w
Herring gull, max. 44w, av. 19w
Amazona parrot, max. 39c
California condor, max. 36w
Domestic pigeon, max. 35c
Canada goose, max. 33w, av. 14w
Military macaw, max. 31c

Domestic duck, max. 31
Cardinal redbird, max. 30c
Domestic fowl, max. 30
Whooping swan, max. 30w
Arctic tern, max. 27w
Adélie penguin, max. 26w
Canary, max. 24c
Caribbean flamingo, max. 23c
Kiwi, max. 20w
Mallard duck, 20w, 19c
European starling, max. 16c, 8w
American robin, max. 13c, 12w
Barn swallow, max. 9w
Budgerigar, max. 8c
Nightingale, max. 7c
Rubythroat hummingbird, max. 5w

Reptiles (in captivity)

Galápagos tortoise, max. 150
American alligator, max. 56
Nile crocodile, max. 40
Gila monster, max. 25
Boa constrictor, max. 23
Reticulated python, max. 21
Snapping turtle, max. 20
Honduran caiman, max. 8

Texas rattlesnake, max. 16
Painted turtle, max. 11
Gopher tortoise, max. 8
Eastern garter snake, max. 6
Tree iguana, max. 5
Mediterranean chameleon, max. 4
Gecko, max. 4
European viper, max. 2

Amphibians (in captivity)

Giant salamander, max. 50
American toad, max. 36c, 15w
Spotted salamander, max. 24
Bullfrog, max. 16

Tree frog, max. 15
Mudpuppy, max. 9
Grassfrog, max. 6
Spotted newt, max. 3

*From Milne and Milne (34), page 311

TABLE II
LIFESPAN OF TREES*

max —maximum recorded age, years
rep —begin reproduction, years
ht —tallest height, feet
diam —diameter at 4½ feet above the ground at maximum size, feet

Bristlecone pine *(Pinus aristata),* max. 4600, rep. 30, ht. 50, diam. 7
Bigtree *(Sequoia gigantea),* max. 3000, rep. 60, ht. 272, diam. 32

Coastal redwood *(Sequoia sempervirens)*, max. 3000, rep. 20, ht. 368, diam. 21
Olive *(Olea europaea)*, max. 2000, rep. 4-8, ht. 50, diam. 3
Bald cypress *(Taxodium distichum)*, max. 1200, rep. 20, ht. 122, diam. 13
Douglas fir *(Pseudotsuga taxifolia)*, max. 1000, rep. 20, ht. 221, diam. 17
Western red cedar *(Thuja plicata)*, max. 800, rep. 15-25, ht. 250, diam. 20
Sitka spruce *(Picea sitchensis)*, max. 750, rep. 20, ht. 180, diam. 16
Sugar pine *(Pinus lambertiana)*, max. 600, rep. 7, ht. 220, diam. 10
Western hemlock *(Tsuga heterophylla)*, max. 600, rep. 20-30, ht. 260, diam. 9
White oak *(Quercus alba)*, max. 600, rep. 20, ht. 100, diam. 8
Western yellow pine *(Pinus ponderosa)*, max. 500, rep. 5-20, ht. 162, diam. 9
Eastern white pine *(Pinus strobus)*, max. 500, rep. 10, ht. 120, diam. 6
Sycamore *(Platanus occidentalis)*, max. 500, rep. 25, ht. 120, diam. 14
Longleaf pine *(Pinus palustris)*, max. 400, rep. 16-20, ht. 120, diam. 4
American beech *(Fagus grandifolia)*, max. 400, rep. 40, ht. 100, diam. 4
Red oak *(Quercus rubra)*, max. 400, rep. 25, ht. 70, diam. 11
White spruce *(Picea glauca)*, max. 350, rep. 10-15, ht. 120, diam. 4
Eastern red cedar *(Juniperus virginiana)*, max. 300, rep. 10-15, ht. 100, diam. 4
Lodgepole pine *(Pinus contorta)*, max. 300, rep. 5-20, ht. 150, diam. 3
Shagbark hickory *(Carya ovata)*, max. 300, rep. 40, ht. 122, diam. 4
White ash *(Fraxinus americana)*, max. 300, rep. 20, ht. 125, diam. 6
Sweet gum *(Liquidambar styraciflua)*, max. 300, rep. 20-25, ht. 200, diam. 6
American elm *(Ulmus americana)*, max. 300, rep. 15, ht. 160, diam. 11
Yellow poplar *(Liriodendron tulipifera)*, max. 250, rep. 15-20, ht. 120, diam. 12
Tamarack *(Larix laricina)*, max. 200, rep. 20, ht. 100, diam. 3
Tea tree *(Camellia sinensis)*, max. 200, rep. 4, ht. 30, diam. 0.5
Saguaro cactus *(Cereus gigantea)*, max. 200, rep. 24, ht. 30, diam. 2
Balsam fir *(Abies balsamea)*, max. 150, rep. 15, ht. 85, diam. 3
Basswood *(Tilia americana)*, max. 140, rep. 15, ht. 125, diam. 5
Flowering dogwood *(Cornus florida)*, max. 125, rep. 5, ht. 50, diam. 1.5
Honey locust *(Gleditsia triacanthos)*, max. 120, rep. 10, ht. 140, diam. 6
Paper birch *(Betula papyrifera)*, max. 100, rep. 15, ht. 120, diam. 5
Quaking aspen *(Populus tremuloides)*, max. 100, rep. 5-20, ht. 120, diam. 4.5
Breadfruit *(Artocarpus utilis)*, max. 100, rep. 8, ht. 100, diam. 3
Apple *(Pyrus malus)*, max. 80, rep. 4, ht. 25, diam. 1
Cacao *(Theobroma cacao)*, max. 50, rep. 4, ht. 30, diam. 2
Coconut *(Cocos nucifera)*, max. 40, rep. 4-10, ht. 100, diam. 1
*From Milne and Milne, (34), page 313

TABLE III
MORE LIFESPAN DATA ON LIVING THINGS*

	Usual Length of Life, years	*Maximum Life, years*
Man	70-80	110 ?
Lion	20-25	40
Dog	10-12	34
Cow	20-25	30
Horse	40-50	62

Pigeon	50	—
Chicken	20	—
Alligator	—	40
Giant Turtle	—	152
Catfish	—	80
Housefly	—	76 days
Fruit Fly	—	37 days
Beetle	—	7-11
Spider	—	7
Sheep	10-15	20
Goat	12-15	19
Camel	25-45	50
Pig	16	27
Elephant	70	98
Owl	—	68
Goose	80	—
Salamander	—	11
Goldfish	—	6-7
Oyster	—	10
Queen Bee	—	5
Ant (worker)	—	5
Earthworm	—	10

*From Birren (40), page 121

Apparently trees also age, though very slowly — much more slowly than the "living" animals. So even trees are not immortal. (Everything seems to die eventually, though the lifespans vary.) Mortal man at 85 years of age has only 10 percent of his cohorts with him; only 10 percent of the original sample is still alive. For the thoroughbred horse, the 10 percent level is reached at 27 years of age; for the laboratory mouse it is one-and-one-half to three years, depending on the strain of mouse (22).

For dogs, the survival curves show that the lifespan of large breeds is considerably shorter than that for smaller breeds. Some researchers have analyzed survival curves for mammals and dogs, coming up with empirical equations which relate lifespan to body weight (10).

Mammals

$$\log x = 0.636 \log z - 0.222 \log y + 1.035$$
where x = lifespan, years
      y = body weight, grams
      z = brain weight, grams

Dogs

$$\log x = 0.60 \log z - 0.23 \log y + 0.99$$

ENVIRONMENTAL EFFECTS ON LIFESPAN

For those of us subjected to a wide range of climatic conditions, individuals from colder locations seem to be longer-lived and slower-growing than those from warm places. For example, some mollusks which were placed in jars at 100 days of age lived for 125 more days at 23°C while at 7 to 20°C, the additional lifespan was 280 days (12). In experiments with rotifers, lowering the temperature 10°C could prolong their lifespan about four times its normal expectancy. Cutting in half their food intake could extend life threefold (44).

This type of information suggests that longevity correlations need to be qualified, bringing other parameters into the description. There are relationships between lifespan and diet, body surface area, weight, metabolic rate, and a dependence has even been found between brain size and lifespan. Birds live longer than mammals of comparable size. Cold-blooded animals live longer than birds or mammals, and it is suspected that these cold-blooded creatures have a rate of aging that is sharply temperature dependent (22).

If I could hibernate and thus lower my metabolic rate, would I live longer? (A bat spends three-quarters of its life hibernating and lives to be 18 years old.) If I lower my temperature, will I lower my rate of living and thus live longer? Table IV supports these ideas, as applied to the water flea and so does Figure 5, which gives some data for the fruit fly.

TABLE IV

TEMPERATURE EFFECT ON LIFESPAN FOR THE WATER FLEA*

Temperature, °C	Lifespan, days
5	4.2
9	11.1
15	14.3
21	9.2
27	6.5
33	4.7

*From Strehler (42), page 68

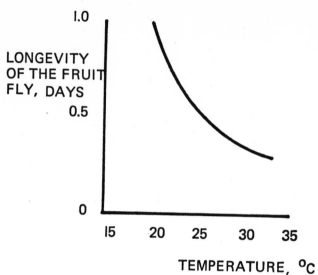

Figure 5. Longevity of the fruit fly with temperature (from Strehler [42], p. 70).

It is interesting to observe from the data in Table IV that there seems to be an optimum temperature for maximum lifespan of the water flea. Depart in either direction from this optimum and the lifespan is diminished significantly. For trout and the droso-phila fly, raising the temperature of their milieu increases their metabolic rate and shortens their lives (41). If I overeat and am constantly well-fed, will my rate of living be higher than usual; and will I therefore live a shorter life than others? (Over-fed house flies are shorter lived than a control group which was fed normally [41].) Does it matter how long it takes me to reach full size; and if it does, can I alter my growth rate by control of my diet? (Small apes take three years to reach full size and live to 10 years of age, while the chimpanzee attains his maximum size at 11 years of age and lives to 40.) The ratio of lifespan to age at full size is about three or four to one (41). Slow the growth, lengthen the lifespan? If a woman is fertile, will she outlive others? (For roaches, higher fertility females have shorter lives than virgin females who lived up to 50 percent longer [42].) Any lesson to be learned here? If there was something to be

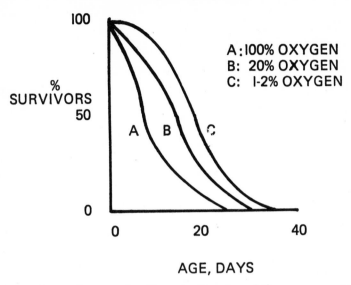

Figure 6. Survival curves for flies as a function of the oxygen concentration in their environment (from Strehler [42], p. 76).

learned, would it be worth implementing? If we are crowded together, as we are in many cities, will we have a shorter lifespan? The answer is yes for the drosophila fly (42). Is it true for us? If I live where the oxygen content in the air is low, can that affect my lifespan? Apparently yes for some flies as shown in Figure 6, where we see that a pure oxygen environment apparently speeds up the rate of living and shortens life. Does this information on flies apply to us in our polluted air? The cynical answer is that the oxygen concentration in the polluted air probably will not be a major factor affecting our duration on this earth — other things in the air will probably do a better job of killing us.

RADIATION EFFECTS ON THE AGING PROCESS

Radiation exposure cuts our growth and weakens our bodies' reaction to injuries. In exposure experiments on animals, the results indicate that a single radiation dose of one roentgen is equivalent in humans to 5 to 10 days of extra age. The radiation also causes increased tumor generation, as if we were older than we really are, when measured by the calendar (40). Neoplasms such as leukemia show up earlier in irradiated mice. Genetic errors are more prevalent after radiation treatment: liver cells of mice show about twice the normal number of chromosome aberrations after a life shortening dose. With radiation, lesions and degenerative diseases show up in small blood vessels and in the walls of the arterioles. Small arteries are thickened with connective tissue. Fibrous connective tissue is found around the walls of the capillaries (33). Curves such as in Figure 7 show dramatically the effect of radiation dosage on lifespan.

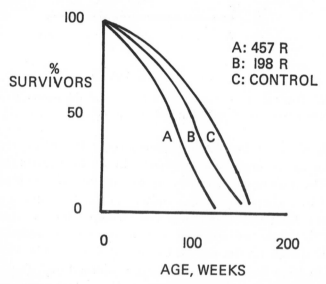

Figure 7.   Effect of various single dosage levels of whole body radiation on lifespan for mice, four weeks old (from Kohn [33], p. 43).

Clearly it can be seen that 50 percent of the original sample are still alive after 120 days for those lucky mice that were the control group and did not get the radiation treatment. For the group that received a dose of 198 roentgens, 50 percent were still alive after 100 days, so they were dying off at a faster rate than the control group. If the mice were exposed to 457 roentgens in one dose, then that group died at an even faster rate, with the 50 percent level being reached after only eighty days. The results speak for themselves. Deaths from malignant cancer in childhood is about 40 percent higher than normal for children who were x-rayed during the last three months of fetal growth than for those who were not (34). Some age groups die more rapidly than others when given this kind of stress, as illustrated in Figure 8. Other investigators found a 30 percent life shortening effect of radiation exposure on mice, but interestingly, the damage they found seemed to be independent of the age of the mice at the time of exposure, as shown in Figure 9. Another way of looking at the pathology of radiation exposure is given in Figure 10, where the incidence of tumors is seen to be increased

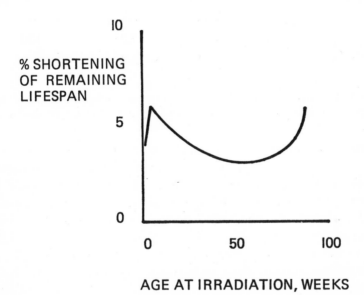

Figure 8. Effect of 100 rad single radiation dosage on mice, showing shortening of life with age (from Kohn [33], p. 143).

dramatically if the irradiation of the mice is done at 20 weeks of age. Whether humans also possess such an age-dependent sensitivity to radiation is not yet known; but based on the mice experiments, there probably is some age in humans where tumor generation is greatly enhanced by some forms of radiation. Figure 11 shows that an increasing dosage raises the mortality rate and also seems to indicate that the nature of the environment during irradiation has some effect on the death rate. Specifically,

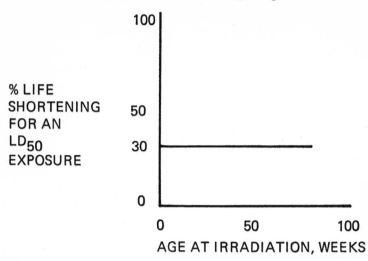

Figure 9.   Life shortening effect of radiation exposure for mice (from Brues and Sacher [36], p. 239). The effect seems independent of the age at exposure (LD$_{50}$ is the dosage which kills 50 percent of the sample).

it would appear from these data that radiation exposure in a pure oxygen environment is deadlier than in air or pure nitrogen. Radiation shortens life by seemingly accelerating the onset of decrepitude. One dies of old age at a young age. Some diseases simulate the effects of radiation, particularly a disease of children called progeria, a rare disease which transforms the young child into an old person in appearance, with baldness, skin wrinkling and coronary disease. These unfortunate children live only about eight years (40).

Low doses of x- or γ-radiation are generally not as effective as high dose rates in shortening the lifespan of animals (6). This implies that the damage, presumably genetic, is a multihit effect; there is a repair process present which can reverse the damage caused by single hits (6). Chromosome aberrations in liver cells of mice caused by irradiation (mutations in the somatic cells) are reversible (9). Radiation life shortening can be induced in adult drosophila flies which are resistant to low doses of radiation by feeding them some amino acids during the larval stage which cause damage simliar to radiation damage (21).

So perhaps a clue to the aging enigma is to be found in the

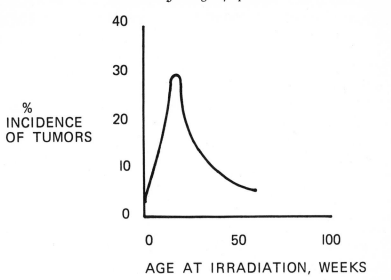

Figure 10. Effect of radiation upon incidence of ovarian tumors in mice at various ages (from Brues and Sacher [36], p. 239).

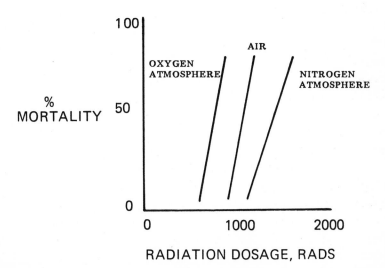

Figure 11. Mortality data as a function of radiation dosage under different gas environments for humans (from Brues and Sacher [36], p. 244).

alteration of cells and DNA by radiation. There are experimental facts which lead in this direction (46):

1. The lifespan of offspring from irradiated male mice may be shortened almost as much as that of their fathers.

2. The effect of a whole body radiation dose of 120 roentgens on lifespan is the same whether the radiation exposure is one dose or divided into doses of 20 roentgens.

3. Immature, developing animals are more sensitive to radiation damage than are adult animals.

4. The lifespan of various species is inversely proportional to the mutation rate of the germ cells.

LIFESPAN AND BODY WEIGHT AND BRAIN WEIGHT

In this area of research there are many people collecting reams and reams of data. Thus, not unexpectedly, we find some correlations between lifespan and body weight and brain weight, as shown in Figures 12 and 13. In examining these figures and

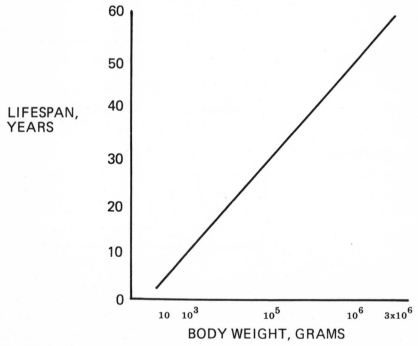

Figure 12. Lifespan versus body weight data for 63 species of animals (from Kohn [33], p. 140).

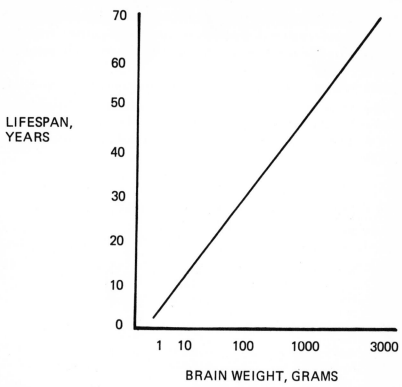

Figure 13. Lifespan versus brain weight data for 63 species of animals (from Kohn [33], p. 141).

finding such neat, simple relationships for pooled data from many different animals, it is very tempting to leap at these generalizations and predict the behavior of one specific individual. But beware: these data are averages for many groups under various conditions and are applicable "on the average," not to one specific individual. Figures 12 and 13 have excluded environmental and genetic factors that may be of more importance than body weight or brain weight as correlators of lifespan. Nevertheless, it is generally true that the heavier animals or those with large brains tend to live longer. There are also relationships between body weight and metabolic rate (and hence between lifespan and metabolic rate). Those species which have high body weights have low metabolic rates (per gram of weight); thus we may infer in a cautious way that if you are an animal with a low metabolic rate, you will live longer. Elephants (heavy, with low metabolic rates) live longer than rats (light, with high metabolic rates).

If you raise the very legitimate question about correlating lifespan with brain weight — that it's not the actual weight that counts, but the brain weight compared to the total body weight that is significant — then you can generate data such as shown in Table V.

TABLE V
LIFESPAN AS A FUNCTION OF BRAIN WEIGHT/BODY WEIGHT*

	$\dfrac{\text{BRAIN WEIGHT}}{\text{BODY WEIGHT}} \times 100$	MAXIMUM LIFESPAN, YEARS
Man	2.67-2.81	80-150
Elephant	1.24-1.34	90-100
Horse	0.43-0.57	45
Bear	0.36-0.50	50
Dog	0.34-0.51	15-20
Crow	0.114	50
Cat	0.29-0.34	20
Squirrel	0.16-0.20	6
Insect	0.06-0.18	6-10
Mouse	0.04	3
Parrot	0.15-0.18	100 ?
Heron	0.046	15

$x = 0.63 \; w + 0.198 \; y + 0.471$ (Reference 36)
where x = log lifespan, years
y = log body weight, grams
w = log brain weight/body weight$^{2/3}$

*From Birren (40), page 124

HEARTBEATS AND DIET AND LIFESPAN

The trends of Table V seem to suggest that brain weight divided by body weight is a rough predictor of lifespan, allowing for some anomalies such as the results for the crow and parrot. We are smugly reassured, at this stage, to note that man has the highest relative brain size of all the animals listed. But in our search for more definite ways of determining the expected lifespan, there is other information available that seems to complicate matters. A mouse heart beats 520 to 570 times per minute. The expected lifespan of a mouse is on the order of three years, which yields over the lifetime of the mouse an expected one billion heartbeats (approximately). On the other hand, an elephant's heart beats only around 25 times per minute. His average lifespan might be 80 years. If we do the same type of calculation as we did before for the mouse, we see that over the expected lifetime of the elephant, he too will have around one billion heartbeats (40). Coincidence? We shall see later that there are other correlations which suggest that perhaps life is programmed in terms of a total amount of energy available, which may be calculated from the number of heartbeats or something else not yet discovered. (In 1908 a theory was presented supporting the finite energy hypothesis. Calculations for total lifetime energy expenditure for horses, cows, guinea pigs, dogs and cats yielded a figure of 29 to 55 million calories per pound weight of the animal. Man, the exception, generated 363 million calories per pound [34].) But it has also been shown that by restricting the diet of immature rats, feeding them nutritious food, but small quantities, it was possible to slow their development, keeping them in a state of immaturity for 766 to 911 days, longer than usual. Then if the caloric content of the diet was raised, the growth rate was accelerated and the rats became mature normally. In the process, however, these special rats had their lives extended about 200 days beyond those who had normal diets (40). Can life in general be lengthened this way? Perhaps. Did the number of heartbeats for the special rats exceed the one billion level expected for the rats with the normal diet? We don't know. But the possibilities are fascinating.

HEIGHT AND WEIGHT AND HORMONES

We don't understand much about the simple process of growth; there are some wide ranges of growth characteristics among living things. For example, can you make anything out of the fact that the pygmies of the Ituri Forest in Central Africa average a whopping 8.6 pounds at birth yet only grow to about six times their weight at maturity (34)? They are human beings, as we are, but this growth pattern is not our expected behavior. Some researchers have concentrated on studies of height and weight measurements as a function of age and other variables in an attempt to understand the aging process. There are all sorts of unusual empirical correlations which can be used as predictors of, for example, our final height (34):

height, in inches = 1.88 x length of the thigh bone, in inches + 32

which is applicable for men. For girls and boys, equations which are good, on the average, for 90 percent of the population are:

girls height, inches = 2 x height at 18 months, inches + ½
boys height, inches = 2 x height at 2 years, inches + ½

We can analyze growth by measuring the height and weight of children. From these experiments it is known that early and late maturing girls have menarche at about the same mean weight, but late maturers are taller at menarche. Two other major events of adolescence: the first spurt in weight gain and the maximum rate of weight gain also occur at invariant mean weights (2). These results lead to speculation that a critical body weight may trigger some adolescent events. Or it may be that during maturation the parenchymal cells continue to grow and fill in the space supplied by the capillary bed until the rate of diffusion of one or more limiting nutrients (or the rate of removal of inhibitory products) prevents further growth (42). We know that the secretion of the estrogen hormone stops female growth. But how? As we grow, we produce more cells; the cells that do not divide get larger. Maggots of the common house fly hatch from eggs with all their cells and generate no more. Their cells simply grow larger and larger with age, accumulate fat, and somehow, when enough fat has been stored, maggot cells cease to grow larger. Having attained this station in life, the maggot has enough sense to stop eating and suddenly a few of its cells begin to divide and differentiate to become wings, legs, eyes, etc. (34). Human brain cells also do not divide, but increase in size and number until we find at age four that 90 percent of the growth of the human brain has occurred, as shown in Figure 14. On the other hand, human white cells die in four days; red cells die in four months (34). Why?

A rough rule of thumb for survival and growth states that lifespan is equal to eight times the age when reproduction is first possible (34). In some cultures they eat the reproductive parts of sacrificial animals in an effort to thwart the aging process, hoping for rejuvenation. Injections of the male hormone, testosterone, can affect the body very dramatically, but this is not true rejuvenation. Brain wave patterns are altered by testosterone, as is the chemistry of respiration and nutrition. The red cell count changes and so does muscle tone. But the effects are not lasting and are reversed when the hormone treatment is stopped. In some experiments, cysteine and folic acid were used for rejuvenation effects, but nothing permanent has yet been discovered (34). I am sure we will hear about it when the secret of the fountain of youth is unravelled. Despite the various treatments which are of some temporary help, we continue to age and suffer from skin thinning (glossy appearance of the skin, wrinkling, a decrease in elasticity, and increased pigmentation),

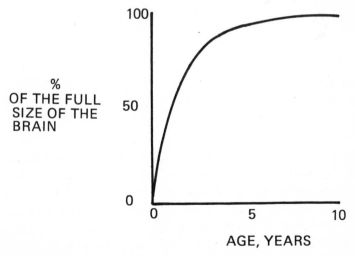

Figure 14. Growth of the brain with age for humans (from Milne and Milne [34], p. 36).

hair loss (and greying and coarsening of the texture), eye cataracts (and changes in lens flexibility), muscle loss (through atrophy), joints less flexible (and swollen), and brittle bones (35).

LIFESPAN VARIATIONS—MALE AND FEMALE THROUGHOUT HISTORY

Some researchers point to the diverse lifespans of various species and say that aging is endogenous and is related to a growth inhibition process which in turn is related to the time when our fixed adult size is attained. Is it clear to you why the maximum lifespan of the house spider should be four days while the longhorn beetle can live to 45 years, the Galapagos tortoise achieves a sensational 177 years of age, swallows only one year, the rhesus monkey goes till 29 years, a chimpanzee can live for 37 years, and the Indian elephant is good till 57 years (40). Superimposed on these data is the fact that females live longer and have lower basal metabolism rates than males. Table VI shows how much longer some females do live. But are they luckier that they manage to survive for longer periods than their male

TABLE VI
SOME LIFESPANS FOR MALES AND FEMALES OF SOME SPECIES*

	Male	Female
Fruit Fly	31 days	33 days
Beetle	60 days	111 days
Spider	100 days	271 days
Rat	750 days	900 days

*From Birren (40), page 231

counterparts? Are they healthy in their old age? Do females live longer because they are subject to different hormonal influences or is it related to the work they do?

The old folks have become an increasing problem for the young as fewer of us die from disease. Though our ultimate, maximum lifespan has not increased very much throughout history, the life expectancy has nevertheless increased, as fewer babies now die at childbirth and as infants. As diseases are eliminated as the cause of death, this life expectancy increases as shown in Figure 15.

The percentage of the population which is 65 years and older has gradually increased as illustrated by Table VII, but

TABLE VII
PROPORTION OF THE POPULATION 65 YEARS OR OLDER*
U.S. 1880 - 1956 (ESTIMATED TO 1975)

Year	% of the Population
1900	4.1
1930	5.4
1940	6.9
1950	8.2
1960	8.8
1975	9.4 estimated

*From Birren (40), page 289

we note that a larger proportion of this older group is female, since females live longer than males. But women reach their final height sooner than men and they tend to gain weight more steadily into later life than their men (40). What does all this mean?

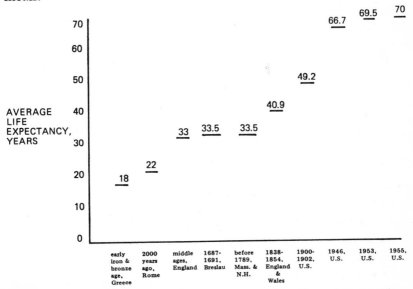

Figure 15. Improvement of life expectancy throughout history (from Birren [40], p. 284).

CHAPTER 2

LOSS OF BODILY FUNCTIONS

ASSOCIATED WITH AN INCREASED SUSCEPTIBILITY to death, old organisms also become increasingly erratic in their responses to their environment (22). Given an upset in temperature, diet, physical activity or emotional stress, the powers of adjustment of the old are weaker than for the younger system. We describe this problem in terms of a diminished feedback response or faulty homeostasis, but the actual reasons, on the microscopic level, are still not known. Why is it that old age robs us of the vitality and control of our faculties?

LOSS OF STRENGTH

For example, in experiments with mice working at elevated temperatures, old rats fared worse than other age groups, as seen in Figure 16. Not surprisingly, mature rats at 200 days of age held up the best.

Old folks seek warmth and complain about severe cold and heat more than younger people. Between ages 21 and 28, the capacity for hard work at high temperatures seems at its best. After age 28, this "strength" falls off sharply. The mechanism for control of heat loss from the body seems to operate less efficiently in the elderly. The frequency of accidents increases for older people, but at elevated temperatures, the trend is dramatic, as shown in Figure 17.

In another set of experiments, rats were bled until they expired. Figure 18 shows some results of this unusual measure of vitality, where we observe that old rats had less survival strength than young ones.

In work capacity experiments on the elderly (turning a crank), the maximum work rate without fatigue decreased about 60 percent between ages 35 and 80. Man's grasp strength of the

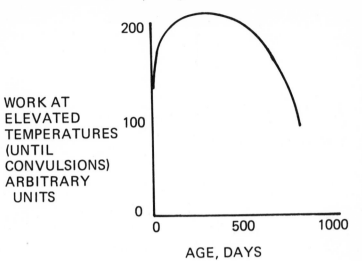

Figure 16. Work at elevated temperatures (until convulsions) for mice, as a function of age (from Kohn [33], p. 121).

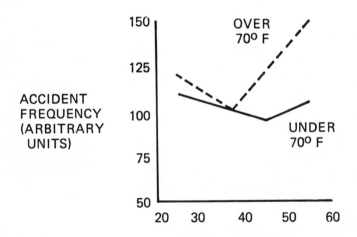

Figure 17. Increased accident rates with temperature for old and young coal miners (from Birren [40], p. 434).

dominant hand dropped about 50 percent as shown in Figure 19, and his endurance in a holding grip was down about 40 percent for the 80-year-old as compared to the 35-year-old man.

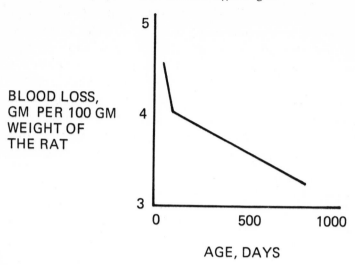

Figure 18.   Blood loss capability before death as a function of age of rats (from Kohn [33], p. 121).

Figure 19.   Loss of strength with age for humans (from Strehler [42], p. 130).

Physical powers decline 30 percent from age 35 to age 70 on treadmill tests, climbing of stairs and cranking on a wheel, but for short bursts, we see the real disability of old age. The peak energy which can be mustered for short bursts of activity drops dramatically: down 60 percent from age 35 to age 70. Is this related to a serious decline in the amount of air which can be pulled through the lungs in 15 seconds (down 40 percent) when comparing a 20-year-old to someone at 80 years of age? Or is old age weakness caused by a drop in blood volume which can be pumped by the heart (from four quarts per minute per square meter of body surface, to almost half that figure between ages 20 and 90)? Older hearts have trouble speeding up to cope with increased activity, and old folks need to take it nice and easy.

As we get older, our collagen (about one-third of the total protein in our bodies) becomes more cross-linked and rigid. We become prone to "collagen diseases" such as arthritis, rheumatism and atherosclerosis (41). Our strength diminishes, as measured by isometric contractions of the muscles of the hand, as shown in Table VIII. We seem to reach our peak strength at ages 23 to 27 and decline thereafter.

TABLE VIII
MAXIMUM ISOMETRIC STRENGTH OF CONTRACTION
OF THE HAND*

Age, years	Strength of the Muscles, kilograms
18-22	53
23-27	56
33-37	53
43-47	50
53-68	46

*From Verzar (41), page 62

Gradually we get weaker as we get older. Athletes know this; they also know that their reaction times are not as good in their thirties as compared to earlier periods. Table IX shows this clearly, where data are presented for teens to 80-year-olds, contrasting their muscle strengths and reaction times. For 17 classes of vigorous sports, a curve showing the decline of our ability (the winning of championships) with age is given in Figure 20. For sports requiring a fine coordination such as golf, Figure 21 traces our loss of ability. It is interesting to compare the two

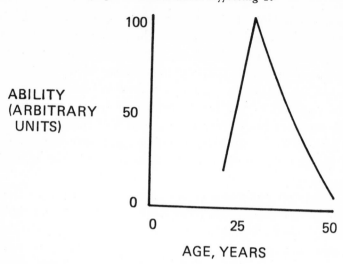

Figure 20.   The decline of ability with age for 17 classes of vigorous sports (from Birren [40], p. 783).

TABLE IX
STRENGTH AND REACTION TIME AS A FUNCTION OF AGE*

Strength
(maximum: age 20-29 = 100)

Age	30-39	40-49	50-59	60-69
Grip, right hand	96.4	90.9	78.0	64.9
Back Strength	95.4	89.8	79.2	64.3

Simple Reaction Times, seconds

Age	teens	20's	30's	40's	50's	60's	70's	80's
Press Key-light on	.228	.201	.201	.217	.212	.217	.245	.353
Brake Reaction	.418	.418	.428	.442	.455	.465		

*From Birren (40), page 568

curves, for we see that for sports which require a fine coordination, the decline seems to come around age 35 whereas for the vigorous sports, age 31 seems to be the age when we are in our prime.

Intellectual skills and productivity are also age related. Thomas Edison had his ups and downs, as shown in Figure 22, but on the whole, he seems to have peaked at age 35 and slipped from there (though he still had his moments at ages

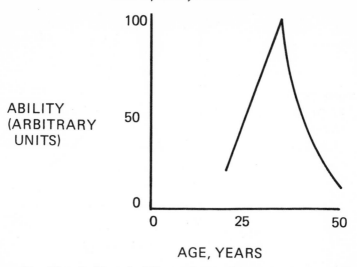

AGE, YEARS

Figure 21. The decline of ability with age for sports requiring fine co-ordination: golf, billiards, bowling (from Birren [40], p. 783).

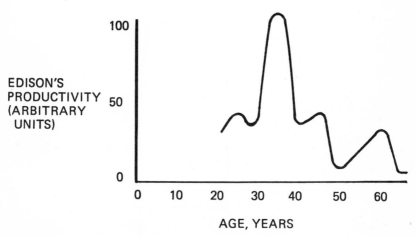

AGE, YEARS

Figure 22. Thomas Edison's productivity (inventions) as a function of his age. Age 35 = 100 (from Birren [40], p. 782).

45 and 60). In studying the productivity of writers and scientists, the zenith of their accomplishments seems to be around age 40, with a rapid decline thereafter, as illustrated in Figures 23 and 24. These curves represent pooled data, so there is hope for us

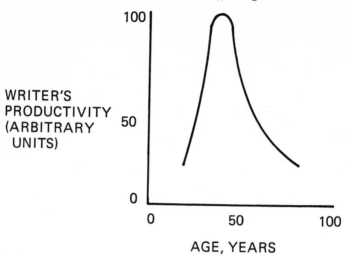

WRITER'S
PRODUCTIVITY
(ARBITRARY
UNITS)

Figure 23.   Literary productivity versus age. Age 40 = 100 (from Birren [40], p. 782).

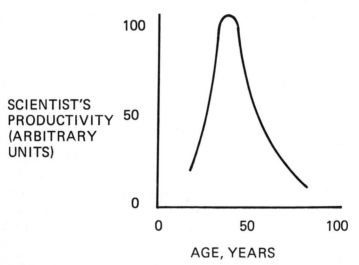

SCIENTIST'S
PRODUCTIVITY
(ARBITRARY
UNITS)

Figure 24.   Scientist's productivity versus age. Age 40 = 100 (from Birren [40], p. 782).

yet if we are over 40. But if you have some great things to do, get to them promptly — your "vitality" is running out.

LOSS OF FUNCTION

In humans, cardiac output, maximum breathing capacity, stomach acid secretion, and "strength" of blood vessels all decline with age. Figures 25, 26 and 27 show clearly that starting with a base of maximum potential at age 20 or 30, we undergo continuous deterioration until at age 70 or so, when we are at low ebb.

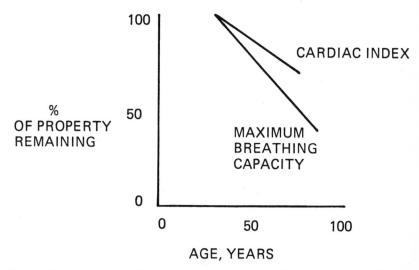

Figure 25. Diminished cardiac index and breathing capacity with age for humans (from Kohn [33], p. 124).

The heart maintains a reasonable capacity in old age, (70%), but breathing capacity is down to 40 percent, and blood vessel strength is down to about 30 percent and is dangerously low. There is a loss in the ability of the lungs to let air through the lung membranes (diffusion capacity); an 8 percent loss in this property for each ten years of life (33).

By the age of 90, the blood volume pumped by the heart is down 50 percent from that at age 20. The elderly take shallower breaths than the young and feel discomfort if forced to breathe more vigorously. For the same blood flow rate through the lungs, it has been found that the man 80 years of age gets one-third less oxygen into his system than the 20-year-old. At 20 years of

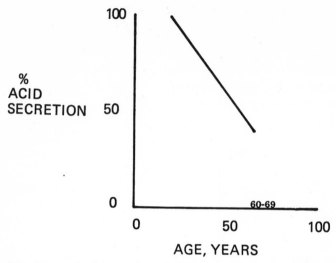

Figure 26.　Diminished stomach acid secretion with age for humans (from Kohn [33], p. 125).

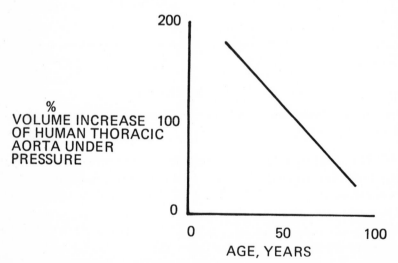

Figure 27.　Diminished strength of the aorta with age for humans (from Kohn [33], p. 127).

age, one-fourth of the blood pumped through the heart goes through the kidneys; at 80 years, only one-eighth of the blood through the heart gets to the kidney (34).

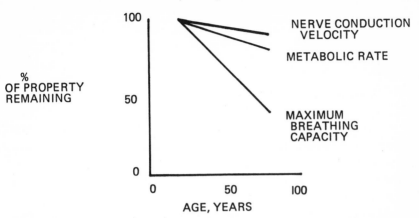

Figure 28. More loss of property data with age for humans (from Strehler [42], p. 96).

More loss of function data is given in Figure 28, which shows that metabolic rate drops with age, as does the conduction velocity of some nerves. How old are you? How old are your lungs? How old are your nerves? How old are your muscles? After age 30, some researchers estimate that we suffer a loss of function of about 1 percent each year. After age 40, the human death rate doubles each successive eight year period. At age 70, the chances of dying are 1 in 18 (34).

Summarizing some of the functional losses with age, as shown in Table X, the melancholy of old age becomes apparent.

TABLE X

FUNCTONAL CHANGES WITH AGE*

Function		% Function at Age 80 (age 30 = 100)
Basal Metabolism—		85
Blood Pressure—	systolic	115
	diastolic	104
Cardiovascular—	cardiac output	65
	total peripheral resistance	150
Respiratory—	vital capacity	60
	maximum breathing rate	40

Urinary—	renal plasma flow	45
	glomular filtration rate	60
Nervous—	conduction velocity	90
Muscle—	hand grip strength	65

*From Bakerman (35), page 7

It is not just a matter of looking old and less attractive; the elderly just aren't functioning very well. Life becomes very tenuous. Relatively small upsets cause catastrophic alterations in bodily functions and there is little reserve vitality to call upon for recovery. And so we die.

We know that our responses are slowed in old age. The "startle" response takes twice as long in the old, speed of copying digits is diminished by 25 percent, the response to a warning stimulation goes from 2.5 seconds to 4.0 seconds. The old need continuous assurance or new information as they proceed in the solution of problems put before them. They reassure themselves by repeated visual examination of the stimulus. More errors are made by the old in translating spatial perception into motor performance. The input and output of information is more tightly coupled in the old than in the young, and it is harder to change the response. An error made is difficult to correct. The old lose speed and flexibility and their reserves (40).

In general, memory starts to fade around age 30. But vocabulary comprehension scarcely changes with time, and old folks, given enough time, will come up with the right answers in decision-making tests. Are these observations related to the loss of brain weight, down from 3.03 pounds at age 30 to 2.72 pounds at age 90? There is no definite answer yet.

The rate of removal of sugar from the blood drops in the old, yielding results which seem to indicate that about half of the elderly could be considered diabetic. After a fatty meal, most of us for two to six hours would be hyperlipemic (excess lipids). For the aged, this condition lasts about 24 hours, which is not too surprising in view of the general slowdown in bodily functions in the elderly (35). Kidney function is diminished, since blood flow to the kidney is only 42 percent at age 70 of what it was at 30 years of age (44). Oxygen uptake in the liver declines from a level of 114 (arbitrary units) in the young to 94 in the old (36). In the brain, there is a decline in oxygen consumption with age, starting with a rapid fall from childhood through adolescence and then followed by a more gradual decline (35). Whether this diminished metabolism of oxygen in the brain is the symptom or the illness is still not known; but we do know that anoxia (a lack of oxygen) will tend to increase the concentration of the old age pigment, lipofuscin, in the neurons (40) so that an interesting question to pose is: Does a diminished oxygen consumption generate the production of these old age pigments or does the presence of the pigments cause the anoxia? In any case, what does seem to be suggested is that we probably achieve our peak brain capacity at age 25 and slide slowly downhill in brain weight and oxygen consumption until about age 70 when senility may begin encroaching upon our faculties.

The endocrine system seems to remain operable at a reasonable level as we evolve towards old age; the thyroid gland function seems to decrease only late in life. The islets of the pancreas do not seem to diminish in number until near the end of life (41). The pituitary hormone levels also seem unchanged with age, but when the pituitary gland in rats is extirpated, they appear to age rapidly and live for one-half to one year at most after that. During this senescent period the rats' growth was stopped, sexual activity ceased, their skin looked aged, hair was lost, and their movements slowed. There was atrophy of all organs (41). Was this an artificially induced aging stress? On the other hand, castration does not seem to influence life expectancy (41). Though some hormonal systems do not change much with age, there is a significant decrease in the secretion of hydrochloric acid and pepsin by the gastric mucosa as shown previously (it is more difficult to digest your food in old age) and a similar loss of activity of some enzymes in the pancreas (amylase, lipase, trypsin). Endocellular enzymes in the walls of the arteries decrease with age (fumarase, coenzyme flavin, and nicotinic acid amine). There is less of the enzyme cholesterolesterase in the liver (41). In general, some enzyme levels change, some do not; and it seems safe to say that catabolic enzyme activity does not change much with age (the breaking down of complex substances into simpler units) but anabolic enzyme activity does decrease with time (a reduction in the production of some proteins by the body [41]).

With age there is a progressive loss of taste buds in the mouth, going from 245 to 88 taste buds per papilla of the tongue as we go from 25 to 70 years of age. Taste buds have been found on the roof of the mouth, walls of the throat, and on the central and upper part of the tongue. By age 10, these are gone and we are left with taste buds only on the front, back and sides of the tongue. These also go with age, and we find our sense of taste diminished. (We put more sugar in our coffee than before.) Young adults sense sweetness at one-third the concentration the elderly require for the detection of sweetness (34), as demonstrated by the data in Table XI which shows that the most sensitive period is the 19 to 50 year bracket.

TABLE XI

SENSE OF TASTE COMPARISON FOR GLUCOSE*

Age, years	Able to Sense the Sweetness of a Glucose Solution of Concentration
7-10	0.68 %
19-50	0.41 %
52-85	1.23 %

*From Verzar (41), page 91

Our eyes get yellowish with age and less transparent; we detect less violet colors. Thus aging artists' sense of color changes, and they tend to use less violet.

Older people need more light to see. While driving a car, older people see less well because they need more illumination. For every 13 years of age beyond age 20, the light intensity must be doubled in order to fully see an object (40). Figure 29 compares the ability of the young and old to see under various conditions of illumination. The peripheral vision of the aged is also diminished (40); even the pupil diameter is different for the old as compared to the young, as seen in Figure 30. By the fifth

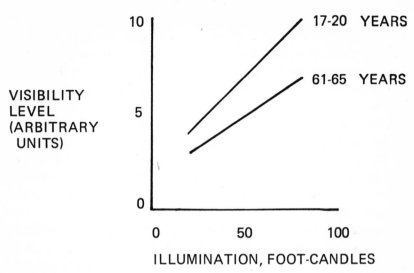

Figure 29. The ability to see at various intensities of illumination for the young and old (from Birren [40], p. 564).

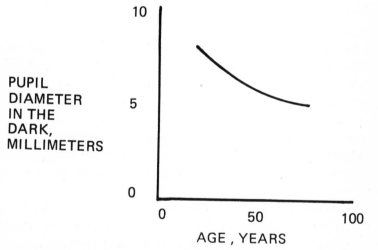

Figure 30. Pupil diameter in the dark versus age for humans (from Birren [40], p. 509).

decade of life, our eyes usually need correction with convex lenses because of a loss of adaptability of the eye lens — it is not as elastic as it used to be (41). Young folks 10 years old can focus their eyes at a near point (shortest distance at which a fixed point can be seen sharply) 10 to 15 centimeters from their corneas; older folks at age 50 can only focus at a near point of 50 centimeters (41). Reaction times for pupil contraction in the eye, in response to illumination, is longer in old folks (41).

Our sense of smell after age 37 is diminished by atrophy and a decrease in the number of nerve fibers (41).

Our sensitivity to vibration (amplitudes of oscillation that can be detected) is dimmed. Old folks need higher amplitudes (stronger vibrations) before they detect the signals, a condition thought to be related to a diminished central nervous function. For example, 10-year-old children can feel vibration amplitudes of 6 microns, while at age 70 it requires an amplitude of 55 microns before the threshold of sensitivity is reached (41). The sense of hearing is diminished by aging of the aural connective tissue and perhaps by a lessening of the number of auditory nerve endings (41): at infancy we hear 40,000 vibrations per second and this is down to 20,000 vibrations per second at maturity (34).

In our searching for what is admittedly a small list of advantages that the old have over the young, we have at last found one: old folks are less susceptible to seasickness than the young. (Their nausea feelings seem to be less intense.) On experiments in rotating chairs, old folks also maintain their "mastery" over the young, suffering a shorter period of dizziness (rotary nystagmus) than their younger competitors (41). These areas of superiority provide small comfort for the elderly.

COLLAGEN AND AGING AND GETTING STIFFER

Old people are shorter than when they were young. Because the cartilages between one bone and the next get thinner, it has been found that by age 60 we are about one-half inch shorter than we were before. By age 80 a male human has lost much of the fat he had on his body; he may be 30 pounds lighter at age 80 than at 40. Women, on the other hand, tend to accumulate fat continuously with age (34).

We get stiffer with age, which is not news for those who try to stay athletic and graceful in their later years. And it has to do with our connective tissue, which in the aged is not as distensible as it was earlier. This connective tissue binds and supports other things in the body, such as the tendons, ligaments, skin, blood vessels, bone, teeth, the lining of the gastrointestinal tract, and the lungs (35). Connective tissue is composed of collagen, elastin and other proteins. As we age, this connective tissue is less extensible; a general feeling of rigidity creeps into our bones. Figure 31 shows some typical stretching results for abdominal skin, where we see that the elderly have less extension or stretching capability in their skin. Table XII gives some of the constituents of connective tissue and defines their functions — included here so that you may know what to blame when you "pull a muscle" trying to do the things in later life that you did easily and quickly in your younger days.

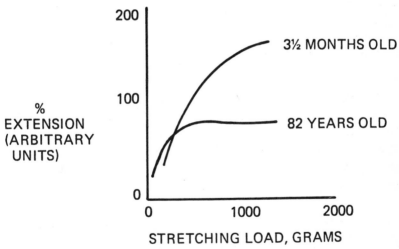

Figure 31. Distensibility of abdominal skin with age for humans (from Bakerman [35], p. 81).

With age, the arterial wall decreases in tensile strength, giving rise to hypertension under some conditions. Tendons become stiffer, more fibrous than before, as the collagen becomes

TABLE XII

CONNECTIVE TISSUE*

Collagen—	in tendons, fascia for locomotion, transmission of force, etc.
Elastic Fibers—	for frequently deformed parts of the body, such as skin, large blood vessels.
Reticular Fibers—	these fibers are finer than collagen or elastic fibers: for intimate support of individual cells in the area of continuous membranes, and basement membranes of the epithelium.
Mucopolysaccharides—	jelly-like substance which coats the surfaces between cells and extracellular space. Lubricates the fibrous elements.

*From Strehler (42), page 139

more cross-linked and hence more rigid and less permeable (35). Calcium levels, which were high at birth and diminished in youth, are built up again in the tissues, producing more rigidity, as illustrated by the data in Table XIII.

TABLE XIII
CALCIUM CONTENT OF ELASTIN (CATTLE AORTA)*

Age, years	Calcium, %
Fetal	.693-.817
2	.125-.500
4	.250-.550
7	.375-.712

*From Bakerman (35), page 110

Plaques of curd-like cholesterol and then calcium nodules develop in the artery walls. The arteries become diseased. The artery walls become less elastic (the elastin becomes more rigid). We deposit ceroid in the elastin fibers and in the cholesterol. Lipofuscin (age pigment) accumulates around the nerve cells and also colors the heart. At age 75, at death, it is estimated that about 3 percent of the body weight is lipofuscin (34).

If the infusion of old collagen causes stiffening of the tissue, is it reversible? Can the old collagen be absorbed and new, young collagen laid down in its place? The answer is not a definite yes yet, but if this old, cross-linked collagen could be replaced, the structural format of an organism would surely become more youthful. Wouldn't the diffusional processes in the parenchymal cells of the tissue and organs become revivified (42)? If a way can be found to break down the cross-linked material and reduce it to excretable components, then people may be able to be rejuvenated. It is known now from experiments with autopsy material that there are substances which can dissolve cross-linked aggregates, but the side effects on living organisms of these substances are not yet established. Estimates are that it will take about ten more years before some useful data is gathered. If these substances are only 10 percent effective, it is thought that human lifespans will be extended to about 150 years. If 20 percent effective humans may live to 200 years (43).

CHAPTER 3

AGING ON THE CELLULAR LEVEL

Is IT THE CELLS that hold the key to life and longevity? Don't the cells contain the information for replication and metabolism necessary for life? If there were a loss of cells in some organ of the body, wouldn't this be important to know? If the DNA and RNA components of the cells were aging and giving erroneous information, wouldn't this be a significant factor in the study of the aging process? Does the brain lose some of its cells, and is this the cause of senility? Is all this related to the increased susceptibility of the aged to cancer? Does the accumulation of lipofuscin and other "old age pigments" in the cells cause aging?

TYPES OF CELLS

In a bacterium, the genes are joined end to end into a single chromosome which is folded over itself. (Chromosome means "colored bodies" because they are easy to stain with the dyes used in cell identification [37].)

There are about 3000 genes in the bacterium cell: these genes are ladder-like in structure and contain amino acids, combined as protein. From one division of the cell, the 3000 genes of the chromosome loop are replicated by enzymes in about 1800 seconds. It is the DNA which specifies and produces the messenger RNA which moves through the cells, spreading the genetic code.

DNA is a double helix organization; RNA is of a single helix structure. Protein synthesis proceeds zipper-like, starting out on one end of the template and continuing step by step (37). It is thought that one gene controls the synthesis of one enzyme (37). Different types of cells have different numbers of genes.

46

For example, a colon bacillus has 3000 genes, a pleuropneumonia-like cell (PPLO) has 40 genes, a human cell contains 60,000 to 80,000 genes (34).

A bacterium cell with its membrane surrounding the nucleus may have a diameter of one micron and a volume of 10^{-12} milliliters. The cell may contain about 3000 different types of large molecules (37). Viruses are of course smaller. It has been said of these living things that their stable state is to be dead — and it is the life process which is unstable (37).

All cells are not alike; they are usually distinguished by specifying whether they are dividing (mitotic) or not. There are fixed, post-mitotic cells which do not divide, are stable and are most differentiated (specialized). They may be nerve cells, red blood cells and muscle cells. Another category of cell is the reverting, post-mitotic cells which may divide again, given the right conditions. Hepatic cells in regenerating livers are such cells and do divide again. The fixed post-mitotic cells such as the nerve cells can live as long as 90 years, which means that they age very slowly, about as slowly or as quickly as the whole organism in which they reside. Recognizing the variability of the aging process down on the cellular level, it is easy to pose some questions about the relationship of cell division and the aging process. Is cell division an attempt to get rid of debilitating elements? Is cell division a mark of a vigorous or declining cell?

There are other ways of characterizing cells such as (33):

Vegetative cells are continuously or periodically dividing cells. Unspecialized primoridal or stem cells, they are the basal cells of the epidermis, hemocytoblasts of bone marrow, and spermatozonia.

Differentiating cells arising from vegetative cells are the specialized erythroblasts and myeloblasts of the red and white blood cells and spermatocytes.

Reverting post-mitotic cells are mature and highly specialized cells, normally non-dividing or rarely dividing. These cells can divide, as is the case with fibroblasts, chondrocytes, endothelial and kidney cells.

Short-lived fixed post-mitotic cells are mature cells derived from differentiating cells. They do not divide (granulocytic leucocytes, red blood cells, keratinizing squamous cells, and mucus acid and enzyme-producing cells of the gastrointestinal tract). They are the epithelial cells which may produce keratin, mucus, sebum or have special organelles such as cilia or flagella. Their shapes and functions are diverse: erythrocytes have hemoglobin and unusual shapes; granulocytic leucocytes have high concentrations of lysosomes; spermatozoa are haploid and adapted for rapid motion.

Short-lived fixed post-mitotic cells such as the red cells in dogs live for about 110 days. Granulocytic leucocytes have half lives on the order of 7 hours in humans. The small lymphocytes of rats survive about 90 days; the larger ones live for about 60 days. Epithelial cells die in about six days in the human male gastrointestinal tract (33). When these cells die, some rupture. Others in death (squamous epithelial) fill with keratin and then are sloughed off from the surface. Red blood cells are taken up by the reticuloendothelial system, fill with hemoglobin, and lose nucleic acid. When leucocytes and epithelial cells die in vitro, their surfaces show beading and pseudopod formation. They absorb water so that some parts become liquid, other parts are gel-like, vacuoles form in the mitochondria, and nucleic acid is found in the cytoplasm. The membranes rupture and release the cell contents (33).

Long-lived fixed post-mitotic cells do not divide. Formed early in the life of an animal, they persist indefinitely and are highly specialized. Some examples of this type of cell are neurons and muscle cells. The differences in lifespan between mammalian cells are enormous: white cells live for hours in humans, neurons and muscle cells live as long as the host. Some researchers think muscle cells and nerve cells do not die as a function of age (33). It has been established that none of the populations of long-lived fixed post-mitotic cells give survival curves typical of an aging population. This suggests that there is no progressive process inside the cell which increases the probability of dying with time (33).

Still another general way of classifying cells is according to their basic stability or permanence (35):

Labile cells form the lining of mucosal cells and hematopoietic tissue. They show mitotic activity and are replaced continually.

Permanent cells are the nerve cells and the myocardium and sensory organ cells. These cells do not divide.

Stable cells are the cells of the liver, kidney and endocrine and exocrine glands. There may be an intermediate turnover rate for these cells; they are replaced when the host is properly stimulated.

CELL GROWTH

Serially cultured human diploid cell strains apparently have a finite lifespan in vitro (3). After a period of active multiplication, generally less than one or two years, it begins to take longer and longer for these cells to generate more cells (initially 24 hours for each doubling). There is a cessation of mitotic activity and an accumulation of cellular debris, and finally the culture degenerates totally. This phenomenon in human fetal diploid cell strains, confirmed in a number of laboratories, goes on for about 50 serial passages in vitro — apparently independent of the media composition or other conditions. Those who believe these results propose the hypothesis that finite lifespans for diploid cell strains in vitro are a manifestation of an aging process, and we are observing senescence at the cellular level. Further, it is said that the changes in cell viability should not be related to calendar time, but to some intrinsic organic time (3).

Frozen human fetal diploid cells stored in liquid nitrogen at –190°C for four years, when reconstituted, will continue doubling until the total number of doublings reaches about 50, a total which includes any doublings done before the cells were frozen. Mixed populations of cells with different doubling potentials do not apparently influence each other (24). Adult cells will only do about 20 doublings, rather than the 50 of the fetal material, seemingly indicating that the adult strains have been subjected to an accumulation of damages which affects their "vitality."

The doubling capacity of cells seems to be inborn. From the data available, there is the expectation that human embryo tissue (lung fibroblasts) can go for 50 doublings. Lung fibroblasts from someone 0-20 years of age can double 30 times, and if the tissue sample is 20 years or older, the capacity is apparently 20 doublings. Shorter-lived vertebrates show less capacity for cell division. For example, normal fibroblasts from embryos of chickens, rats, mice, hamsters and guinea pigs double no more than 15 times in cell cultures. (The adults have doubling potentials of less than 15.) In one series of experiments, male human fibroblasts which had already undergone 40 doublings were seeded with female fibroblasts which had divided only 10 times. Most of the males doubled 10 more times (for a total of about 50), and all the males were gone after 25 more doublings. These types of experiments seem to indicate that aging involves some sort of depletion or dilution of a cell's chemical or "vital" resources, and perhaps these elements are fixed at birth and are consumed with time (28).

During the active proliferation period, the karyotype of human diploid cells is stable, but in the senescent stage there are chromosome aberrations and aneuploidy. Dividing mammalian cells may yield daughter cells which are unequal in age. Studies with protozoa do not support the usual assumptions of unicellular animal immortality or that the outcome of a protozoan cell division is a pair of rejuvenated infant cells. (There is some support for the idea that protozoan cell division yields a mother cell as well as a daughter cell [24].) Amoeba seem to multiply indefinitely if kept on an optimum food supply. But if kept on a limited food supply and then transferred to the optimum diet, they have a variable lifespan (30 days to 30 weeks). Conjugation experiments with protozoa have not yet yielded definite conclusions; some clones were rejuvenated, others were not. Based on these studies, we may cautiously say that death is not a result of multicellularity (24).

The cells which are most likely to divide for long periods in vitro are fibroblasts (24). Least likely to divide extensively are post-mitotic or highly differentiated parenchymal cells. But if there are comfortable explanations for this behavior, we ought to now interject some deflecting ideas: abnormal cells in vitro seem to proliferate indefinitely. Apparently malignant cells can avoid senescence in vitro and in vivo. These cells in vitro yield tumors (and cancer and indefinite growth) when transplanted in vivo. On the other hand, diploid cells in vitro, on transplantation in vivo, yield normal somatic cells with finite growth histories.

A cell colony of chick fibroblasts will not survive long in vitro, but normal mouse cells cultured in glass vessels can undergo spontaneous transformations which enables them to divide and multiply indefinitely (28). Human cells called HeLa, obtained from cervical tissue in 1952, are still growing and multiplying. These are abnormal cells, having 50 to 350 chromosomes per cell (mixoploid cells) compared to 46 chromosomes in normal diploid cells. These transformed HeLa cells behave like cancer cells and will grow as tumors when inoculated in some laboratory animals. Normal human cells can be routinely transformed into cancer cells by exposing them to the monkey virus SV-40 (28). Transformed cells in a series of tissue transplants from animal to animal will grow indefinitely while normal cells will not. For example, normal mouse skin can survive only a limited number of serial grafts from one mouse to another.

One way of doing these serial culture experiments is to take some tissue (such as lung tissue fibroblasts), break down the tissue using trypsin enzyme, centrifuge the mixture, collect the cells, and put them in a nutrient medium. Incubate the cells at 97°F on a glass surface where the tissue grows again. Then repeat the steps with this new tissue. By this method it was possible to take fibroblasts from a 4-month-old human embryo and go through about 50 growth stages until the cell population died (after about six to eight months of experimentation). If the process was interrupted and then resumed, the same total number of growth stages were obtained. One could freeze the cells and hold the operation for six years, and when the proper growth conditions were restored, the cells resumed their doubling. They seemed to remember, for the total number of doublings still came to about 50 (28). Figure 32 shows how a cell population grows by doubling and then ages and dies.

As the population of fibroblasts nears the end of its lifetime,

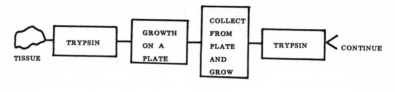

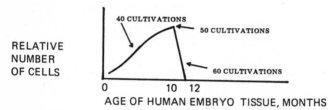

Figure 32. Growth and regrowth of tissue by serial cultivations (from Hayflick [28]).

aberrations show up in the chromosomes. Leucocytes and liver tissue of mice show similar changes. It should be pointed out that these are in vitro experiments with little or no evidence to connect with in vivo behavior. But we do know that the human brain weighs less in old age than in its prime, that the kidney loses nephrons, and that the taste buds of the tongue disappear in the aged. Cells in vivo do age, die and disappear. We know that the larval tissue of insects and the tail and gill cells of the tadpole stop dividing, age and die with age (28).

So we can speculate: Is the death of cells a normal, programmed event for multicellular animals? Is life (aging) programmed? Is there an analogy between aging of living systems and the wearing out of machines — such as the ultimate death of an automobile, where we can calculate its life in miles? If we accept the machine analogy, then perhaps we can say that the aging process results from a deterioration of the genetic programs which orchestrate the development of cells. The DNA of dividing cells may become clouded with an accumulation of copying errors (like the "noise" in copying a photograph). Certain enzymes in DNA which make protein may deteriorate with age. Man may live longer than animals because human cells have a more effective system of correcting or repairing errors as they arise. Can we therefore set up a scale of lower to higher forms of animal life based on the ability to correct or repair errors in the cells? And can this be correlated with lifespan? Is the longest living animal representative of the highest form of life?

SENESCENCE

At the cellular level there seems to be at least three aging processes (28, 35):

1. A decline in the number of non-dividing, highly specialized cells such as nerve and muscle cells.

2. Progressive stiffening with age of structural protein collagen (which is present as about one-third of all body protein and is in the binding substance of skin, muscles and the vascular system).

3. A limitation on cell division (such as the fibroblasts) and degenerative mutations in successive generations.

Some of the cellular degenerative alterations found in permanent cells are (35):

In the nucleus there is clumping, shrinkage, fragmentation and dissolution of chromatin. We find inclusions in the nucleus and some enlargement and invagination of the membrane.

Mitochondria are decreased in number with an alteration of shape.

The Golgi apparatus shows fragmentation.

No gene in the chromosome exerts its influence until there is an information flow from the DNA in the cell to the RNA molecules. The RNA is the template from which are generated new materials in the cell. Outside influences may disrupt this process. For example, some chemicals which are excreted by various organs of the body can dramatically affect the cells. Obtained from the thymus gland, a material called retine has been found to retard growth; conversely, a substance termed promine can promote growth. Retine can also be obtained as an extract from edible mushrooms, giving some credence to the folklore which said that mushrooms were good for cancer victims. Similar properties are ascribed to the quahog, a common variety of clam from New England. Some growth is thought to be controlled by chemicals which contain sulfhydryl groups. Also, by a mechanism which is not known, radiant energy at short wavelengths (ultraviolet rays of sunlight, x-rays or radioactive materials) can cause cancer. Viruses are also thought to cause cancer, by probably producing transformations on the cellular level. Large viruses, such as the cold virus, have been found to cause cancer in laboratory rodents; a small virus, polyoma, causes cancer in mice. The common wart of human skin is a benign tumor caused, it is believed, by a viral invasion (34).

Some investigators suspect that as the cells divide, mutations (errors) begin to crop up in the hereditary, replicating activities of the genes and the DNA. By age 90 we probably carry one mutated characteristic in every cell and we become very vulnerable to distortions in our life processes. Red blood cells are apparently subject to mutations on the order of 100 to 1000 times more frequently than egg cells or sperm cells (34).

Can we delay the senescence which may be caused by mutations? Those who grow plants indoors know that in some plants they can postpone senescence and death by trimming away reproductive parts. Some indoor plants can be maintained in a rapid, juvenile growth state if each flower cluster that forms is pinched off before the blossoms open. From these results we can tentatively conclude that at maturity, we go into a decline by perhaps producing hormones or something that initiates the aging process. Others suggest that in a living organism it is the gamma globulin (with its antibodies) in the lymph nodes, spleen, liver, etc. that in later life yields mutated antibodies and white cells which attack their host's cells (34).

Cell counts do change with age in some organs and not in others (35). For example, in the brain there is a decrease in neurons of the cerebral cortex and a 25 percent loss in Purkinje cells of the cerebellar cortex. So the brain ages by, among other reasons, an apparent loss in the number of non-dividing cells. On the other hand, the liver seems able to regenerate or maintain its cells. The kidney glomeruli, like the brain, seem to show a decrease in the number of cells they possess.

In the cells that do not divide, such as those in the brain

and muscle, the DNA is thought to be renewable, at least partly. Over a period of 115 to 800 days the DNA in the brain cells is replaced with new DNA. As the DNA is replaced, errors in synthesis can occur, thus introducing mutations and possibly then promoting the aging process (35). Experiments have been performed on mouse livers in an attempt to verify the presence of genetic damage in old age. The mice were treated with carbon tetrachloride, which damages the liver cells. After the treatment, the liver was allowed to regenerate; and the cells were examined for damage to the chromosomes. Figure 33 shows that old mice produced more chromosome aberrations than did young mice.

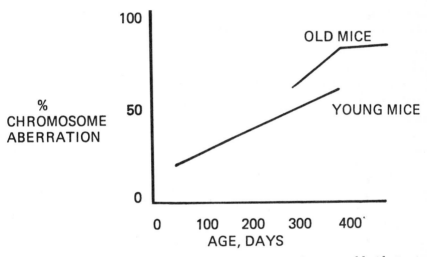

Figure 33. Chromosome damage resulting from carbon tetrachloride treatment and regeneration of the liver (from Bakerman [35], p. 41).

One of the first signs of age in tissue cultures is the presence of fatty granules or vacuoles in the cell protoplasm (40). Eventually these granules and vacuoles completely fill the protoplasm and cytolysis develops (35). Age pigments (brown or yellow in color), thought to be degenerative waste products, replace active cytoplasm and seem to be associated with senility. Experiments on animals with vitamin E deficiencies show similar pigmentation results (35).

Old age pigments such as lipofuscin granules are found in old heart muscle and in spinal ganglia of senile rats. Lipofuscin production can be artificially stimulated by injections of cortisone or by subjecting the animal to low oxygen environments. If this is done in young rats and then this artificial stress is removed, the aging effects are apparently reversible, for the lipofuscin disappears (42). In older humans, the lipofuscin can accumulate at a rate of about 0.3 percent of the total heart volume per decade of life, as shown in Figure 34, where at age 80 the old age pigment amounts to about 5 percent of the heart substance.

Some explanations of the aging phenomenon raise the suspicion that perhaps the accumulation of waste products has something to do with aging. These waste products are thought to accumulate because of a decrease in the permeability of our cell membranes, and this is thought to be related to an increase in the amount of calcium we store with age. Others, along this same vein, propose that toxins arise from intestinal purification.

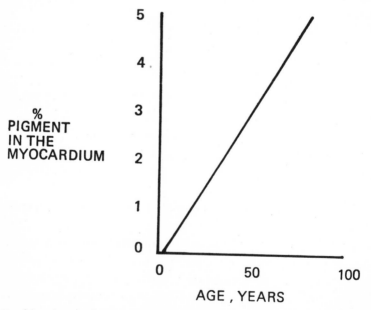

Figure 34.   Accumulation of lipofuscin pigment in the myocardium heart muscle with age for humans (from Strehler [42], p. 186).

One researcher in 1908 even decided to live on sterile rolls and Bulgarian sour milk (rich in lactobacillis) in order to alter his intestinal bacterial flora. He died at age 71 (40).

Cells that lose their capacity to divide ultimately disintegrate (skeletal cells, cardiac muscle, nerve cells, the ova of the ovary). With age, the fibers of the crystalline lens of the eye cease to undergo mitosis and show similar changes with age as does collagen. In connective tissue, not only does the collagen age by cross-linking, but so do the fibroblasts, which become collagen fibers (41). We know something about vitamins and old age and cell behavior. We know that ascorbic acid, vitamin C, is essential for the production of collagen and without vitamin C we get scurvy; the teeth become loose because of a lack of collagen in the gingiva and fall out. This leads to some interesting speculation pertaining to the dosage of vitamin C required for good health (41).

If we can see the aging phenomenon on the cellular (microscopic) level, will we be able to understand the way it works? In the cells of young mice we find many mitochondria. With age, the mitochondria appear as large granules: a characteristic of a senile mouse is to have large granular mitochondria. This granularism is also found in Purkinje cells of the cerebellum. Neurons may also contain altered mitochondria (42). So is the basic aging process related to the mitochondria? One can study oxygen consumption of mitochondria from tissue homogenates, as given by Table XIV, and find that oxygen consumption diminishes markedly with age. Are the cells running down? With

TABLE XIV

OXYGEN CONSUMPTION OF GUINEA PIG KIDNEY HOMOGENATES*

Age	Oxygen Consumption (microliters per milligram N per hour)
Young (8 weeks)	18.61
Middle (51 weeks)	11.04
Old (100 weeks)	7.44

*From Strehler (42), page 174

age, there is an increase of aneuploidy in the liver tissue of dogs, guinea pigs and rats (42). Does this aberrant condition contribute to the aging process? Does it cause the aging process to proliferate throughout the rest of the body? Is this alteration in the chromosome condition occurring simultaneously in all the cells of the body? Why?

One of the tragic results of a disturbance in the orderliness of chromosome replication is mongolism, where we find that there are extra, small acentric chromosomes in the cells. Table XV traces the incidence and hence the probability of finding mongolism in the newborn as a function of the age of the mother.

TABLE XV

INCIDENCE OF MONGOLISM IN THE NEWBORN AS A FUNCTION OF THE AGE OF THE MOTHER*

Maternal Age, years	Average Incidence (arbitrary units)
15-19	23
20-24	24
25-29	25
30-34	71
35-39	220
40-44	829
45	2080

*From Strehler (42), page 179

Obviously there is a greater risk of mongolism in the baby when the mother is older, raising questions about the age of the egg from which came the child.

Red blood cells arise from the bone marrow. They age as they circulate in the blood vessels and at some key time they are replaced by young cells from bone marrow cell division. Whether the replacement rate is related to the age of the host animal is not yet known. We do know that serum or plasma from old animals can inhibit cell proliferation in tissue cultures. In old animals, some stem cells seem to be "poisoned" by some as yet unknown inhibitory factors, as indicated by the data given below (33) which shows that it will take longer for old tissue to grow in a new environment. Some think this trait of older cells is related to latent viruses, mutations in DNA, slow accumulation

Chicken Heart	*Tissue Transplant Donor Age*	*Latent Period Before Cell Growth Takes Place*
	4-day embryo	4.9 hours
	8-day embryo	5.5 hours
	14-day embryo	9.3 hours
	18-day embryo	11.0 hours

of harmful substances, diluting out of some cell component that cannot be reproduced at a sufficient rate, and perhaps even to some factors introduced by the experimental techniques (33).

Red blood cells live only about 120 days in the body. They are produced by erythroblasts, whose mitotic activity decreases with age. Old people produce young, new red blood cells just as young people do. But the new cells produced in old bodies are slightly different from the new cells generated by young people (41). Red cells which achieve an age of about 120 days are recognized in the body as being old and are rapidly broken down. It may simply be a change in the specific gravity of the old cells or perhaps a change in mechanical strength or resistance to osmotic lysis (a change in membrane permeability) that causes the disintegration of the old red blood cells. With age, there is a decrease in the ATP levels in the red cells which may be another factor causing their automatic demise at about 120 days (42).

Tracer techniques allow us to determine the lifespan for red blood cells (29). Blood stored in a glucose medium at 4°C deteriorates after a few days, with the loss in ability to metabolize glucose, loss of potassium ions from the cells and replacement with sodium ions, increased osmotic and mechanical fragility, and a deceased ability to survive when transfused into a recipient.

The maximum, permissible, in vitro storage time for whole blood is 21 days, when 70 percent of the red blood cells will survive after transfusion (29). Obviously something goes wrong in the cells, related perhaps to the degradation of the phosphate esters of ATP. Some researchers suggested that we add ATP to a failing cell culture but this proved ineffective. The ATP couldn't seem to get through the cell membrane. Other investigators suggested adding nucleosides to stored blood (in the manner sketched in Figure 35) and suddenly the storage time was no longer 21 days but 40 to 50 days, and some of the cell lesions were reversed. Is the deterioration of a red cell related to an aging process? And if it is, have we hit upon a therapeutic approach for the moderation of the aging phenomenon?

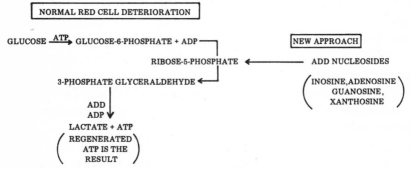

Figure 35.   Scheme for adding ATP to the red blood cell and extending its in vitro storage time (from Huennekens [29]).

Studies of non-dividing cells leads naturally to the brain and its relatively stable cell population. But our brains do age, and in particular, our brains lose weight with age, as shown in Figure 36. The loss of weight of the brain after age 25 may be associated with a decrease in the number of brain cells, or perhaps it may be that the water content of the brain is diminishing. (In old brains, it has been observed that there are shrunken, dried out Purkinje cells present.) There are other measures of old age in the brain. Some researchers find "senile plaques" in the grey matter of the brain which may result from the precipitation of inorganic products from the aged, altered extracellular

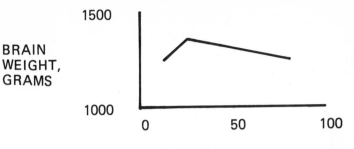

Figure 36.   Loss in brain weight with age for humans (from Birren [40], p. 137).

material (40). As we age, the solids of the brain, presumably the intellectual material, slowly decrease as seen in Figure 37. Though the solids content of the brain appears to decrease with age, the DNA content, in seeming contradiction, increases after

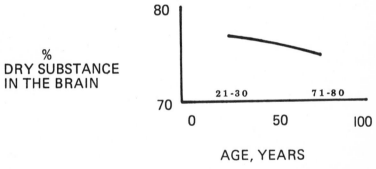

Figure 37.   Loss of dry (solids) material in the brain with age for humans (from Birren [40], p. 197).

age 31 to 40, as shown in Figure 38. This is believed to be caused by an increase in pyknosis of the neurons and the growth of glial cells. It is thought that the human brain achieves its peak development around 30 years of age, then declines (40). Age 70 is chosen, on the average, as the time for the onset of senescence, for then the moisture content of the brain increases rapidly (40). Is this the "softening of the brain" that some of us attribute to our friends?

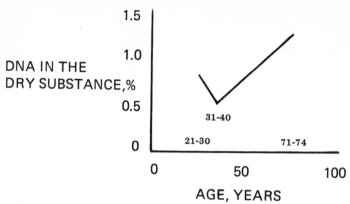

Figure 38. Increase in DNA content of dry substance of the brain with age for humans (from Birren [40], p. 200).

REGENERATION

Do the cells of an organ of the body regenerate if there is some loss of cells? One researcher (34) implanted an inflated plastic pouch in place of a diseased bladder. In less than two months the first tissue layers of new bladder had grown. In three months a coating of smooth muscle tissue enclosed the inner layer, and soon the bladder regeneration was completed. The 3-inch by 4-inch plastic bag was then deflated and removed through the uretha. The nerve connections seemed good.

In the liver, only one of 10,000 to 20,000 cells is in mitosis at any time (33). If one of the lobes of the liver (about 70 percent of the liver) is removed, the remaining cells proliferate rapidly and reconstitute most of the original liver in a few days. Young rats can regenerate liver tissue more rapidly than adults (33).

If there is some regeneration possible on the cellular level, doesn't this indicate that some aspects of the aging process are reversible? Young, middle-aged and old rats can apparently regenerate liver material equally well, but old rats do not produce as many cells containing nuclei as their younger brethren, suggesting that the new mass produced by old rats is not as functional as the new material generated by the younger ones (42). Experiments on the muscles of rabbits seem to indicate that some muscle regrowth is possible: the researchers ligated the blood supply of the gastrocnemius muscle of some rabbits and found that the muscle material was soon broken down and resorbed. Then the researchers restored the blood supply; after some further degeneration, there was a regrowth phase where new muscle was deposited. Soon nerve cells appeared and the muscle became functional — nearly as good as before (42). How is this possible? Why can't it be done in other animals and other parts of the body? Is there a need for a connective tissue frame upon which to build the new material? Some muscle tissue can be regenerated, but the process is not fully understood. Is this regeneration of tissue related to the observation that in the old there is greater time lag before a wound begins to heal than for the young (42)?

Salamanders can regenerate lost toes; sometimes they can even replace a foot. The cells beneath the scar tissue regain their embryonic state capabilities, begin to divide, and restore the original tissue patterns of the lost member. Soon the tissue has specialized as new bone, connective tissue, muscles and skin through which blood vessels extend themselves. Nerve cell regeneration is much slower. Earthworms regenerate as long as no serious injury is caused to the region between segments 4 and 30 where the vital organs are located. There are 180 segments in the body of an earthworm and when some segments are lost, they can be regenerated exactly (the same number are produced to replace those which were lost [34]). Is this ability to replace lost portions of the body a sign of a higher order of life? Humans can't do what the salamander or the earthworm can do — yet.

In a human cell there are 46 chromosomes in the nucleus of each cell. Cell division (mitosis) takes about one day. A second division also takes about one day; subsequent divisions are slower. Nerve cells don't divide; skin cells do divide. Cancer cells that result from mitosis fail to align themselves smoothly against neighbors or to form neat mosaics. Instead they pile on top of one another. When about 10,000 cells are clumped, then we see a tumor. It takes about 12 divisions starting from one cell to produce a noticeable lump. Cancer cells take about six days for each division; after 150 days there could be a mass five-thirty-seconds of an inch in size which is formed, the result of about 25 divisions (34). This is not the sort of regeneration we seek.

INFORMATION THEORY

There may be something more fundamental operating on living things than that which has been presented up until now: something which may govern the aging process and ultimately be able to define life. Organisms can be considered islands of orderly structure; if this is true, then aging may be an increase in randomness or disorderliness. A failure of the buffering power of the living system to control the upsets encountered may scramble the information stored in the chromosomes. Some say that this disorganized information (noise) can accumulate in the cellular information system. Stresses that scramble the chromosome information on this cellular level, such as radiation, seem to accelerate the aging process. Those who push this point of view even suggest that the background radiation we all encounter on earth may be a factor in aging. This hypothesis has fascinating possibilities, suggesting experiments where whole animals are raised in radiation-free environments for a number of generations. Would these animals after a few generations begin to live forever?

Aging may be caused by a loss of cellular information brought on by (21):

(1) Random damage caused by the accumulation of chemical noise.

(2) Irreversible switching off of genetic processes which synthesize needed materials.

Random damage may be caused by radiation-induced cross-linking and colloid changes, free radical effects, or the release of lysosomal DNA enzymes.

Talk of randomness and information content leads researchers to the concept of entropy, which can be roughly defined as a measure of the disorder of the system. Those who hew to this line of reasoning say that the force of mortality is dependent not only on time, but also on some physiological equivalent to the wearing out of an automobile (even though we continue to replace its parts as it wears out). In other words, there may be some innate property of the whole organism related to the disorder (entropy) generated by the organism which is responsible ultimately for the death of the living system. Death may come when the level of this generated disorder reaches some critical mark; or it may be a cumulative thing, with death occurring when the summed total of this disorder or entropy achieves another critical level (22).

CHAPTER 4

DEATH AND
DISEASE-SUMMING UP

IN THE ELDERLY THE SKIN WRINKLES, is rough, and may have pigmented areas and warts. There is a loss of subcutaneous fat, a decrease in the elasticity of the connective tissue, and loss of hair from the head and face. Old skin tends more to malignancies than young skin. The thickness and volume of the epidermis decreases with age, there is a decreasing number of glomus units and a loss of sweat glands (42). In the vascular tree, coronary arteries, and aorta, we find fatty plaques and fibrosis, with calcium and other metallic ions bound in the region of the fibrosis. From these deposits, blood clots, lesions and hemorrhages can occur, as well as stiffening of the walls of the vessels (42). Old beef has more old collagen and is tougher.

Aging and death criteria are not always so simple to define. On the cellular level, it is difficult to define the absolute death of a cell, for it may disappear as a result of a number of changes: (1) aging and then death; (2) fission (splitting) into two or more units; (3) coalescence of two or more individuals, as is done by slime molds; (4) change in constituent parts, such as the replacement of subcellular constituents or the replacement of cells as they wear out (42). When parenchymal cells die out, they are replaced by fibroblasts, with a subsequent loss of function. Even our nervous system seems to lose some cells, which may be a clue to our dysfunction with age (42).

On the macroscopic level, considering the organism as a whole, the causes of death (the apparent reasons) vary, depending on the quality of the medical care. As can be seen in Table XVI, for the year 1900, the leading cause of death in the United States was pneumonia; but by 1959, after the advent of

penicillin, pneumonia was down to sixth place on the list, affecting mostly the elderly. Absent from the list is the fundamental
cause of death: old age.

TABLE XVI

THE LEADING CAUSES OF DEATH IN THE UNITED STATES
FOR 1900 AND 1959*

1900	% of all deaths	1959	% of all deaths
Pneumonia	11.8	Heart Disease	38.6
Tuberculosis	11.3	Cancer	15.7
Diarrhea and Enteritis	8.3	Cerebral Hemorrhage	11.5
Heart Disease	8.0	Accidents	5.4
Cerebral Hemorrhage	6.2	Early Infancy	4.1
Nephritis	5.2	Pneumonia	3.5
Accidents	4.2	Arteriosclerosis	2.1
Cancer	3.7		

*From Strehler (42), page 116

In studying death rates, factors such as where the studies
were done, who the sample population was, and when the data
were collected become important, as illustrated in Figure 39.
Today these curves would be essentially the same, but there
would be fewer deaths in the early years.

Death is said to occur when demand surpasses the ability
to expend energy; the stresses of everyday life are supposed to
be distributed in the same way that the energy of gas molecules
in motion are classified (33).

At least 90 percent of all deaths are partly caused by the
decline in vitality which occurs with age (43). Of a sample of
100,000 men at age 20, only 100 would be expected to die within
one year; whereas the same number of men at age 80 would lose
20,000 of their cohorts. If cancer were to be completely eliminated, some say that our life expectancy would be increased by
only about 2.5 years; others are more generous and think our
lives would be extended about 15 years (43). If cardiovascular

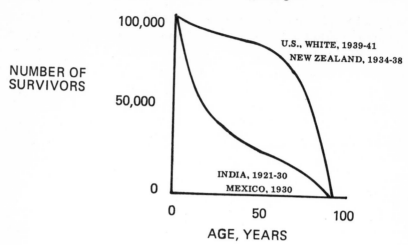

Figure 39. Death rate for humans caused by diseases, accidents, etc. showing differences in population, location and when the data were collected (from Kohn [33], p. 107).

diseases were gone, the extension in lifespan would be ten years. But ultimately we would still die. How long would you live if all diseases were eliminated and all accidents never happened? And no one killed anyone else? You would still die. There is something more basic working on the life process, and some believe it is related to entropy.

We do know some general concepts which help to put our knowledge of the aging process in perspective (33):

1. Differences in lifespan reflect genetic differences, shown by family and twin longevity data and studies on different species.

2. Physiological variables (cardiac output, muscle strength, etc.) decrease steadily with age: at 90 years of age, these parameters are about half of their values at age 20.

3. Old age pigments, which are thought to be chemically inert in the body, accumulate with advancing age in long-lived cells such as heart and muscle cells.

4. Cancer incidence increases with age.

5. Underfeeding leads to an increase in lifespan.

6. Mortality rates are proportional to age.

7. Exercise in 16-month-old rats increases the conduction velocity of their nerve fibers from 51 to 70 meters per second, which suggests that exercise is one way to help a living organism to function better than it might ordinarily. Even old rats were able to improve their conduction velocities by exercise, from 20 to 45 meters per second.

8. Debilitating characteristics of old age appear when growth ceases.

9. Laboratory animals given whole body radiation early in life recover but tend to lose their hair, look worn out, and die at higher rates than the control group which did not suffer the radiation exposure.

In summary, we have dealt with the question of longevity and mortality, aging and dying. Obviously much work has been done in experimentation on animals and people on the macroscopic (whole body) level as well as on the microscopic (cellular) level. We can describe those changes which tell us that we are indeed getting older and approaching death, but we do not as yet understand why and how this aging process begins and continues.

[PART II]
WHY WE DIE

CHAPTER 5

AGING THEORIES IN GENERAL

N⁰ ONE HAS YET PROPOSED and proved that there is one primary reason for aging and death. Many theories have been presented, to be sure, but each proponent of this theory or that theory usually comes to his conclusions from his own frame of reference, from his own prejudice, from his own data.

Aging processes manifest themselves in a number of ways, affecting different parts of the organism differently. This leads to one categorization of aging (33):

Chemical aging — there is an increase in crystallinity (of the eyes), a decrease in solubility of some materials (lipofuscin deposits in the heart), increasing cross-linkages (of collagen), polymerization and denaturation of long chain protein (giving mutations), and mechanical wear and tear.

Extracellular aging — this level of aging involves mostly the connective tissue (fibrous protein, collagen, reticulum, elastin, mesodermal cells, fibroblasts). Old elastin is frayed, fragmented and brittle (33). There are losses in the hyaluronic acid level which affects water distribution in the body (33). The gels become hydrated; mucopolysaccharides are synthesized and degraded.

Perhaps you are one who believes in free radical-caused degeneration or cellular wear and tear, or colloid deterioration or the running down of the tissue (nervous, vascular and connective). Or you may belong to another group of believers who ascribe aging to the toxic waste products of metabolism, cumulative damage of radiation, the running down of energy or entropy, or the depletion of critical materials. You may believe in cell senescence, which includes the loss of irreplaceable enzymes and somatic mutations as possible causes of aging. Or you may say that we age because there is senescence of the gonad-pituitary hormone regulation of growth (1, 40).

Some of the aging processes may be functional, such as the protection of epithelium afforded by the generation of keratin. But other accumulations are not thought to be useful — such as lipofuscin pigments induced by tissue hypoxia and vitamin E deficiency (33).

You may believe that it is the accumulation of these inert deposits in the cells and organs which causes the aging dysfunction. So-called old age pigments such as lipofuscin may be the culprits or perhaps it is calcium, deposited in an uncontrolled way that is the problem. Rats rendered calcified by a high fat diet can regain their youthful appearance if we tie up their calcium with vitamin D and then remove this material by precipitation with ferric chloride. But can old, naturally calcified rats have their disease reversed in this manner? Not yet. Is the deposit of calcium or lipofuscin the cause or the result of the aging process (35)?

Some suggest that there is irreplaceable matter for us to consume in living; and upon its depletion, we die. Thus lifespan is related to our "rate of living" or "vitality" (defined as our ability to restore our organs and cells to their original, normal conditions). Others are more concerned with the cumulative effect of our rate of living and say that the sum of all the stresses and resulting damage leads to aging and death (35). We know that cells die, organs lose cells with age, and that normal diploid somatic cells seem to die after about 50 divisions. Neural impulses are transmitted more slowly as we age, finally becoming disorganized and beyond repair. Hormones dramatically affect aging symptoms, but the effect is not lasting (35).

One of the popular theories of aging, autoimmunity, suggests that with age some alterations occur in the body's immunological defense reaction, and the host attacks its own kind. Do the molecules change with age and become foreign, and hence attacked, or is it the defense mechanism itself which undergoes the pathology? And how does this appear as an aging process (35)? Or do you subscribe to the somatic mutation theory of aging (related to autoimmunity) which hypothesizes that by alterations in the nucleic acid structure, the somatic cells mutate, possibly forming "old" cells prone to disorganization and death.

Aging theorists talk of cross-linking and collagen and the possibility that collagen ages, becomes more cross-linked, rigid and less permeable. Thus the theory suggests that the bodily processes slow down or are progressively hindered with collagen deterioration. Find a way to remove old cross-linked collagen and lay down young collagen and you've discovered the secret of the fountain of youth (35). Radiation is thought to be a non-chemical cross-linker and a free radical producer (35). So there seems to be a connection between cross-linking theories and radiation and free radicals. Perhaps these ideas are connected with DNA and RNA on the microscopic (cellular) level. If this is true, perhaps there is only one "real" theory of aging which encompasses all of these ideas.

One of the benefits of all these theories of aging is that they generate suggestions for experiments which may confirm or deny the hypotheses. For example some enzymes administered orally seem to remain active, thus allowing research dealing with the relationship of enzyme level and aging. Feed the animal the hormones and enzymes which seem to be depleted with age and stop the aging process (36)? We are a few years away from a significant step in this direction since there are only a few of these substances which can be injected into the living system and reach the desired metabolic site without being denatured. Autoimmunity and free radical buffs are working with chemicals which suppress immunological sensitivity and neutralize free radicals, and they are trying to measure any changes in the aging rate. There is danger in these experiments, for if the animal is stripped of its immunological defense, it is vulnerable to other agents which may kill it. The proponents of somatic mutation as a theory of aging need to find a way of removing the mutated tissue once it is identified (35). Not too much success has been obtained so far; but if you allow that radiation is a mutator, then some anti-radiation chemicals (some sulfhydryl compounds and serotonin) may be effective in removing mutated cells. But what do you do about cosmic radiation and other ambient radiation sources?

Some researchers have attempted to dissolve globulins which seem to accumulate with age in liver tissue and replace them with soluble globulins (35). Can this be done more generally, treating other old age insoluble accumulations? At this time we cannot dissolve lipofuscin and other old age pigments without deleterious effects on the organism, but it would seem that this avenue of research is worthwhile. And will we find that the side effects are more destructive than the old age we are trying to ameliorate?

There is an obvious relationship between aging and dermatology. The skin readily shows the loss of irreplaceable cells or enzymes from the cells, becoming rough, and on the head, leading to white hair or loss of hair follicles. It is the skin which shows the obvious changes in its clonally dividing cells, leading to benign and malignant growths. It is the skin which also shows changes in collagen and elastin, so that our skin becomes less elastic. All of these changes appear to be sensitive to radiation, drugs, hormones, emotion and infection (23).

There is also an obvious relationship between aging and information theory on the cellular level. There is a connection between aging and the failure of some feedback mechanisms (27). The problem of dyshomeostasis may be in the nucleus information store or in its transcribing mechanism, which may be repairable. The repair of informational "noise" may be chemical in nature or may involve gene interactions. There may also be selective deletion of informational nonsense through some metabolic activity — characterized by a rising oxygen uptake — in an attempt by the sick cells to compensate for the increased production of nonsense materials (27).

Before going into the details of some of the more favored theories of aging, we still need to review a few of the seemingly unconnected ideas, which when finally collated, will help to explain or confirm some of the theories. So once again we summarize still another researcher's favored list of parameters which govern aging (20):

1. We accumulate harmful metabolites such as collagen.

2. Wear and tear stresses take their toll.

3. Mutations in somatic cells accumulate harmful genes, which cause cells and organisms to function less efficiently.

Along with his list, this investigator (20) lists his observations which seemingly contradict or cast doubt on the theories he has offered us. He notes that skeletal muscle shows little accumulation of fibrous tissue and other products of a deranged metabolism, and yet muscles show marked aging changes. (One of the first signs of aging is a loss in muscular ability.) He further notes that wear and tear experiments on mice have not been successful in proving anything and that the mutation theory is not easily verified, though radiation experiments do seem to show that the aging process is accelerated by irradiation. In support of the mutationists, we are offered the observation that organs with cells which divide frequently (skin)age very slowly but where the cells divide seldom (liver, kidney, heart) the organ is seen to age readily. Why is the mutation rate for somatic cells in plants and animals higher than for gametic cells? And isn't that a lucky break?

Still another set of theories from another researcher are (23):

1. Vigor declines because of a change in the multiplying cells (epidermis), by an accumulation of faults, or faulty copying in clonally dividing cells.

2. Vigor declines through loss or injury to non-multiplying cells (neurons and muscle cells).

3. We age because of changes in inert materials such as collagen.

4. We age because of somatic mutation caused by radiation among other things.

5. We age because of changes in DNA on the molecular level, leading to the production of wrong messenger RNA.

6. Aging is related to the level of nutrition: if fish are underfed, their growth rate is retarded and they live longer than usual. For Wistar rats, their gain in life is proportional to the severity of underfeeding. Starvation for one day in three or four produces a 20 percent increase in lifespan for the male Wistar rats (only a 15% increase for females). The retarded rats have the

appropriate cell population for their size group, not their age group. In other words, it is the number of cell divisions that is being limited by dietary means. At the same time, in these experiments it is found that some of the irreplaceable cells, which are already in place at an early age (such as in the brain), may be protected by this procedure so that we see less degenerative disease than would be expected if we were comparing groups by age classification only. Basal metabolism is higher in these retarded rats, implying that they are also younger if compared to a peer group on the basis of basal metabolism correlations.

7. Aging is a progressive loss or deterioration in the fixed post-mitotic cells.

8. Aging is a stochastic (hit or miss) proposition. By a fault in the inherited pre-zygotic condition (a miss) or by an acquired post-zygotic event (a hit), we lose or deactivate two similar chromosomes and then lose the cell which contains the chromosomes. The lost cell is replaced by extracellular fluid or connective tissue.

9. We age by an autoimmune process, caused perhaps by a breakdown in the mechanism which normally stops leucocytes from producing antibodies which attack its own body constituents. Thus the mutation is in the antibody producer, not in the host cells, which is the usual assumption in the other theories. (Theories which predict cell-by-cell death are criticized on the grounds that the predicted aging process is too slow.)

What is needed is a theory which says that one cell's damage leads to its neighbor's damage, and that there is a single set of mechanisms, morphogenic in the fetus, developmental and defensive during maturity and responsible for aging and senescence in later life. But we are not yet perceptive enough to discover the overall truth about the aging process.

We continue to list some pet theories of aging (30):

1. The colloidal theory says that there is an analogy between aging of inorganic colloids (Jello®, for example) and biological aging, where both systems seem to dry out with age. The colloid theory proponents suggest a cross-linked structure as the reason the material becomes more resistant to enzyme action.

2. The philosophers who push the energetic theory for aging propose that lifespan is inversely proportional to metabolic activity.

3. The pessimists suggest an intoxication theory, guessing that toxins accumulate with age and interfere with bodily functions.

4. Somatic mutation is on everyone's list of aging causes. The theory says that we suffer deleterious mutations in our cells.

5. The autoimmunity theory is a masochist's dream, for it proposes that our own body attacks itself after a while, devouring itself through ill-design and ill-function, or perhaps through a pre-set signal or stimulation.

6. The free radical theory is one of the most favored these days and because of this, we shall devote much more to it later. For the moment it is sufficient to say that free radical reactions are ubiquitous in the living system. Free radicalists hypothesize that these chemical constituents called free radicals adversely affect the living organism; and one can invoke data from whole body radiation tests, experiments involving vitamin E deficiency, oxygen toxicity, and others to support the hypothesis.

He died of "old age" is one of our favorite expressions, but what does it mean? Helplessly we respond with unproved theories, for all we know now is that old age encroaches upon all of us with no exceptions. But we do know that, somehow, senescent tissue provides a favorable environment for diseases. So let us continue to list the things we know, in the hope that perhaps something will sort itself out (31):

1. Organs like skeletal muscle show little accumulation of deleterious products of metabolism — yet with age they show marked changes in ability and strength.

2. Stress does take its toll, but may not be a significant factor in the aging process.

3. Some believe that cells are endowed with a given amount of enzymes when the organism is formed, and these enzymes are exhausted in the living process.

4. Somatic cells of mammals develop chromosome aberrations at high rates — gametic cells seem to be protected.

5. Spontaneous mutations are caused by errors of replication. But non-dividing cells also develop mutations.

6. Offspring of old mothers have more defects and shorter lifespans than do those born of young mothers. The age of the father does not seem to be a factor. (We know that ovacytes, which can exist for a long time without cell division, do accumulate mutations, while male spermatozonia undergo cell division continually and do not seem to build up mutations.)

Finally, before we deal with the more favored theories of aging in some detail, we provide a list of still another researcher's prejudices (33):

1. Latent viruses cause aging.

2. Lipofuscin pigment in muscle cells and neurons is the culprit.

3. Wear and tear takes its toll.

4. Random hits or mutations cause the problems of old age.

5. Free radicals upset cell function and age us.

6. We lose our immunity and our antibodies tear us apart.

7. We accumulate inert or harmful material with age and this causes malfunctions.

8. Big molecules become cross-linked and diminish our bodily functions and produce decrepitude.

Who do you believe?

What do you believe?

CHAPTER 6

SOME FAVORED MICROSCOPIC THEORIES OF AGING

THE FREE RADICAL THEORY OF AGING

THERE IS NOTHING INHERENTLY FREE about free radicals. As a matter of fact, free radicals are costly, if you believe that free radicals are a cause of aging. But what is a free radical?

In considering chemical reactions, we generally speak of substances gaining electrons (reduction) or losing electrons (oxidation) when they react. A free radical is a chemical specie which has been involved in an oxidation reaction and has gained or lost some of its normal complement of electrons. The free radical, which is also present in the organic oxidative processes of the body, is very reactive and disruptive. It is present on the cellular level where the aging sequence may be initiated — which is one of the reasons the free radical theory of aging is so attractive.

Free radicals may be generated by the oxidation of organic compounds as illustrated below.

$$RH + O_2 \xrightarrow{Cu} R^{\bullet} + HO_2^{\bullet}$$

where

R   = organic chain
H   = hydrogen atom
O_2 = oxygen molecule
Cu   = copper catalyst
$R^{\bullet}$ = organic free radical
$HO_2^{\bullet}$ = inorganic free radical

This reaction is apparently followed by others such as

$$R^{\bullet} + O_2 \rightarrow RO_2^{\bullet}$$
$$RO_2^{\bullet} + RH \rightarrow R^{\bullet} + ROOH$$

81

where

$RO_2^\bullet$ = an intermediate organic free radical

ROOH = a new organic material generated by the reactions

Then finally

$$R^\bullet + R^\bullet \to R{:}R$$

where

R:R = condensed product of two $R^\bullet$ free radicals

The net result of the free radical chain reaction is an oxidation of organic material by molecular oxygen, where the organic material, RH, is converted to free radicals and other compounds. Not all of these new products are usable or desirable. Some disturb the fine workings of the cells and thus the free radical theory supposes that by these reactions, the seeds of our own destruction are constantly being generated in the normal course of living.

Free radicals insinuate themselves into our lives by routes other than metabolic reactions, arising from such diverse possibilities as:

1. The reaction of oxygen with gasoline in automobile engines.

2. Smog formation.

3. The drying of linseed oil paints.

4. The rancidity of butter.

5. The formation and production of plastics.

Within living systems, these omnipresent free radicals are believed to cause many deleterious effects, categorized generally by the list below:

1. Cumulative alterations of collagen, elastin and chromosomal material.

2. Breakdown of mucopolysaccharides through oxidative degradation.

3. Accumulation of metabolically inert material such as ceroid and age pigments through oxidative polymerization reactions involving lipids, particularly polyunsaturated lipids and proteins.

4. Changes in membrane characteristics of mitochondria, lysosomes, etc., due to lipid peroxidation.

5. Fibrosis due to irritation caused by peroxidation products of serum and wall components (probably lipids).

Free radicals react with DNA, causing unstable intermediate products which then alter the DNA molecules and interfere with the coding of genetic information. Thus the damaged DNA may continue to function, giving mutant products; or the RNA may be the aberrant part of the chain; or it may be that the enzyme which produces the RNA may be damaged. A wrong protein generated may cause immunological reactions or alterations in cell properties or loss of nutrients or an excess of waste material — all factors which are important in the aging process.

The free radicalists, in order to cement a unique position in the hierarchy of aging theorists, place free radical effects centrally and crucially, as shown in Figure 40.

Effects of Radiation

Radiation produces free radicals by interaction with cellular water to form hydroxyl radicals, hydrogen ions, and electrons. Radiation doses sufficient to kill one-half of the people exposed to it produce only one free radical in every 10 million molecules exposed, so the free radical proponents stress forcefully that free radicals must be potent disrupters of the life process (49). Only slightly less damaging are the lipid peroxidation free radical reactions, which are about one-tenth as destructive as direct radiation (49).

A single radiation exposure of 1000 rads (lethal for most mammals) could yield about .000001 millimoles of free radicals per gram of weight of the organism (45). In living systems, cosmic radiation and other background sources may subject us to a radiation dosage approximately equivalent to 0.1 rad per year (46) or one roentgen of x-rays. This low dose rate produces about .0000001 moles of free radicals per human body per year (45). Can this constant, ambient level of radiation produce a low level of "naturally occurring" mutations in a specie? The chromosomes which control cell reproduction are extremely

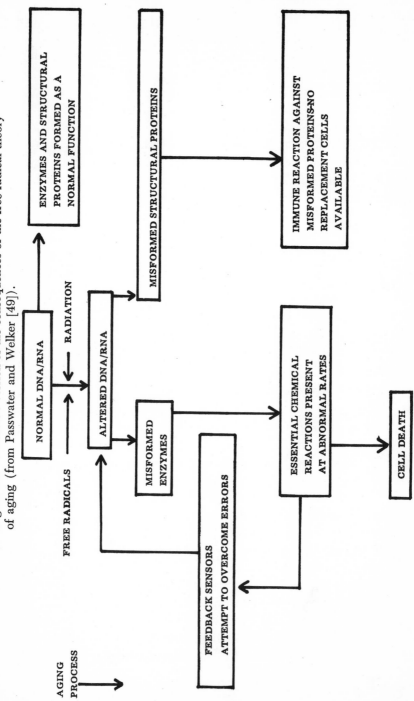

Figure 40. Schematic version of the consequences of the free radical theory of aging (from Passwater and Welker [49]).

sensitive to radiation though the cytoplasm in the cell is much less affected. It is estimated that if one molecule per million in a cell is destroyed, the cell may die. Based on these data, it would seem that background cosmic radiation and other radiation sources could produce a constant source of evolutionary mutations. Radiation may also induce cross-linking of the macromolecules of the living system, which can lead to a fouling of the workings of the organism.

And are mutations, evolution and cancer all part of the same design — radiation and free radicals influencing living, metabolizing organisms (46)?

Effects of Oxygen

In the cells it may be metallic ions, enzymes and cellular materials which, together with oxygen, produce free radicals and initiate destructive oxidation processes (45). Oxygen reacts with serum lipoprotein constituents and arterial wall lipid deposits to form products that may be involved in arteriosclerosis. If oxidation of lipids plays a significant role in arteriosclerosis, then the serum concentration of copper (a good oxidation catalyst) should be found to be elevated in those with the disease. Data to substantiate this hypothesis was obtained and did support the idea (5):

Age Of Those With A History Of Myocardial Infarction	Serum Copper Level
46.5 years	133 micrograms per 100 ml sample
Control (43.4 years)	123 micrograms per 100 ml sample

There are other types of free radical reactions: it has been shown that DNA upon irradiation forms radicals (45); and perhaps because of this, amino acids or fragments from them can be incorporated abnormally into DNA.

The free radical theory of aging deals primarily with the mechanism of oxygen utilization by the cells. Though degraded by oxygen, living systems also require oxygen in order to metabolize food for survival. So we have a mixed blessing. If the cellular system were rigorously organized, oxygen would be utilized only in the enzyme reactions within the cells and under strict control, but this is not the actual case. We know that this available oxygen is consumed in a way that gives rise to peroxides which produce free radicals — leading to some random, uncontrolled and disruptive chemical reactions inside the cell. Nature does exercise some moderating influence on the aberrations, and we observe that within the cells there are naturally occurring antioxidants which neutralize some of the free radicals and prevent catastrophic side reactions. The proponents of the free radical theory of aging contend that despite the presence of some naturally occurring antioxidants, there is nevertheless a continuous, though small, production of free radicals throughout our lifetime, which causes damage and aging. Some of the cell damage may conceivably be repaired by the organism, but the cumulative effect is what we call the aging process. Some researchers suggest that the membranes are the key to survival, for it is through the cell membranes that the substances for life maintenance must pass. And it is in the membranes that the greatest and most critical damage is rent by the free radicals (45). Membranes contain unsaturated lipids which are more oxidizable than proteins; and since it is through the membranes that oxygen diffuses, some say that it is logical to look to the membranes as the controlling influence in the aging process.

In the mitochondria, an oxidative process goes on which most researchers believe involves free radicals and also coenzyme Q, which is related to the chemical family of quinones. The mitochondria, the major sites of cellular oxidation, use large amounts of oxygen but are protected from the harmful free radical reactions by vitamin E, an antioxidant. Experiments which supplant vitamin E with coenzyme Q in the treatment of some vitamin E deficiency diseases have reversed the disease, suggesting that coenzyme Q is involved in the antioxidation process, acting as a free radical scavenger and hence a moderator of the free radical reactions (45). It is known that the chemical structure of vitamin E and coenzyme Q are similar.

The free radical theory of aging is well established, but there is not yet a definitive study which shows that synthetic antioxidants or massive doses of vitamin E will increase the lifespan of humans (45). There are data which show that the lifespan of mice can be increased with antioxidants, but do these results apply to humans as well? And surely we must beware of the possible side effects of these chemicals, ingested in relatively large amounts.

Effects of Vitamin E

Some antioxidants when fed to mice have apparently been a factor in extending their lifespan. Speculation on why these chemicals are effective in prolonging life range from their antioxidant properties as free radical scavengers, to their ability to help increase the formation of essential enzymes in the cells.

The discussion of oxygen and its toxicity and of antioxidants and their palliative effects leads quite naturally and relentlessly to vitamin E, which is supposed to possess antioxidant properties. Polyunsaturated fats are oxidized readily in the body; if this reaction is allowed to proceed at an unhindered rate, it can lead to serious diseased conditions. This potential is moderated by the presence of vitamin E, and some investigators have found a correlation between vitamin E needs for health and the fraction of the fats in the diet which is unsaturated (45). For example, too high a level of unsaturated fats in the diet can lead to sterility in rats, but this condition can be prevented by raising the ingestion level of vitamin E. Similar data have been presented for some forms of brain degeneration and creatinuria.

In many studies, a direct connection was found between excess lipid oxidation (lipid peroxidation) and the degree of the vitamin E deficiency. We also know that the rate of oxidation of lipids in a cell is faster when the cells contain unsaturated fatty acids. Since vitamin E is an effective antioxidant, the logic of connecting lipid oxidation, unsaturated fats, free radicals, vitamin E, and aging is apparent. There is some disagreement as to whether vitamin E acts specifically as an antioxidant or only as one of the participants in the antioxidation process. And it may be that there are other chemicals which act similarly. Some materials have already been identified, with long chemical names; but the toxicity and side effects of these free radical scavengers (antioxidants) are not fully established. Thus we tentatively add to our lexicon of chemicals which have been used as substitutes for vitamin E in the treatment of some diseases brought on by vitamin E deficiencies (45): coenzyme Q; diphenyl-p-phenylene-diamine; 2,6-di-tert-buty-4-methoxyphenol; 1,2-dihydro-6-ethoxy-2,2,4-trimethylquinoline (ethoxyquin); and methylene blue.

Some of the data obtained using vitamin E substitutes are conflicting, suggesting to some researchers that traces of vitamin E are required for these substitutes to be effective. Another complicating factor in these studies is the realization that there are different forms of vitamin E. Thus one form of vitamin E (γ-tocopherol), abundantly present in corn oil, is effective in protecting red cell membranes from excessive oxidation damage, but it is only 10 percent as effective as another vitamin E form (α-tocopherol) in another application (45). The need for vitamin E in human nutrition is established; but there is some disagreement on the amount required, which is not surprising since we know that there are a variety of species of vitamin E, as shown in Table XVII.

TABLE XVII

VARIOUS FORMS OF VITAMIN E AND THEIR BIOLOGICAL ACTIVITY*

	Biological Activity in International Units (IU) for 1 milligram of Vitamin E
dl-α-tocopheryl acetate	1.0
dl-α-tocopherol	1.1
d-α-tocopheryl acetate	1.4
d-α-tocopherol	1.5
l-α-tocopherol	0.5
β-tocopherol	0.1
γ-tocopherol	0.1
δ-tocopherol	very low

*From Pryor (45).

The recommended daily dosage of vitamin E is: infants, 5 IU; children 1 to 10 years of age, 1 to 15 IU; adults, 20 to 30 IU. A study done in 1965 (45) showed that our daily intake of vitamin E varied from 3 to 15 milligrams, with the average intake being 7.4 milligrams; if these data are correct, it would appear from Table XVII that some of us are not getting enough vitamin E into our systems. We know that the need for vitamin E depends directly on the amount of polyunsaturated fats in the diet and we also know that cooking tends to destroy the vitamin E content in foods. Some chronic disorders may be the result of a vitamin E deficiency and may be treated with large doses of vitamin E. (Large doses of this vitamin are not considered harmful.) Some researchers advocate a vitamin E intake of a few hundred IU's per day, with claims of beneficial effects in the treatment of diseases such as atherosclerosis, some heart conditions, diabetes, ulcers and muscular dystrophy (45). There is some preliminary evidence linking vitamin E to cholesterol levels in the blood.

The free radical theory of aging also connects with another theory of aging involving the production of age pigments such as lipofuscin. This colored material which seems to be inert and may be harmless metabolic debris, accumulates with age in tissue, especially in the heart and brain cells (45). It is believed that lipofuscin results from lipid and protein fragments which are generated by the peroxidation (excessive oxidation) of the cell membranes.

Effects of Ozone

Elevated pressures of oxygen produce cellular damage and death, apparently by increasing the rate of lipid peroxidation: vitamin E protects mice from hyperbaric oxygen disabilities. Other compounds such as mercaptoethylamine, glutathione, cysteine, propyl gallate, also are effective free radical scavengers in ameliorating high pressure oxygen effects, extending the life-span of mice in a six-atmosphere oxygen environment. Some researchers are more concerned with the pathological damage caused by ozone and suggest that ozone produces lipid oxidation and organic free radicals and is responsible for some pulmonary and non-pulmonary diseases we suffer in smog (which has a high ozone concentration).

At sea level, the normal ozone content of air is on the order of 0.02 parts per million which is a concentration high enough to do some cellular damage to living systems (45). But levels as high as 0.2 to 0.3 parts per million are not uncommon in Los Angeles, where a 0.6 level has been reached; In smog we may expect 0.5 parts per million. Levels of 10 to 15 parts per million of ozone can kill small mammals in several hours. Rats exposed to 3 to 15 parts per million of ozone die off at a faster rate if they are vitamin E deficient (45). Ozone also makes our response times slower. The normal level of ozone, 0.02 parts per million, could produce .000001 moles of free radicals in the body per day. Thus ozone, beneficial to the extent that it screens our earth from excessive ultraviolet rays, may initiate damaging reactions in the body. As we produce more and more air pollution, we inexorably increase the ozone concentration in the air. Vitamin E protects mice against the lethality of ozone and mammals against the toxic properties of high oxygen pressures (45). Some sulfur compounds protect against ozone effects and the oxidative disruption of nitrogen dioxide which is also in smog.

Additions in the Diet and Life Extension

If the presence of free radical scavengers in the cells affects the aging process, then by measuring serum mercaptan levels, we should have a clue as to life expectancy. (Mercaptans are free radical scavengers.) People with high serum mercaptan levels could expect to live longer than those with lower values; those with low mercaptan levels should die faster. Vitamin A, niacin and vitamin C have properties much like the mercaptans, and we find that old people (who die at a faster rate than younger people) generally have low blood concentrations of these chemicals (8). It would seem that we are on to something here, which could lead to a way of extending life.

The activity of free radicals is enhanced by catalysts such as copper, iron and manganese and inhibited by the antioxidants which remove the free radicals. Polyunsaturated fats react more rapidly with oxygen (giving more free radicals) than do the saturated fats while the amino acid tyrosine is more reactive than another amino acid, phenylalanine. This suggests that we might choose our foods critically with the aim of decreasing the potential level of free radicals. We might add antioxidants to our diet and minimize our intake of polyunsaturated fats. For example, by feeding, some mice a diet containing 0.5 percent butylated hydroxytoluene (BHT), it was possible to increase the age at which 50 percent of the mice were dead by about 50 percent. (In humans this is equivalent to extending life expectancy from 70 to 105 years.) Conversely, if we increase the content of unsaturated fats in the diet of some strains of mice and rats, their rate of dying increases. We know that copper accelerates free radical reactions and whether coincidence or not, we note that human serum levels of copper increase with age and males with a history of coronary artery disease have higher serum levels of copper than those with no history of coronary disease.

It has been demonstrated that the concentration of free radicals increases with increasing metabolic activity, which makes sense if free radicals are actually involved in oxidation reactions (46). In studies with vitamin E deficient animals, the mitochondria and microsomes are found to contain lipid peroxidation products (46), arising by a free radical path. (Cells with a normal amount of vitamin E would also be expected to produce lipid peroxidation products but at a slower rate.) The continued survival of living things in a changing environment results from a sorting out of the energy reactions available and an accommodation to the side reactions (and resulting mutations) caused or accelerated by free radicals. Thus it would seem logical to link free radicals, evolution, mutations, cancer and survival.

Diet additives are assumed to act diffusely within the organism. On the other hand, external free radical producers such as radiation are targeted at more specific locations in the body and would not be expected to produce experimental results similar to those obtained with the food additives. The mechanism by which free radicals produce their effects, while still somewhat obscure, is thought to be operative in the mitochondria. The free radicals could initiate oxidation-polymerization reactions involving unsaturated mitochondrial lipids, which could give rise to the old age pigments and cause other changes in the mitochondria (46). The free radicals would also be expected to react readily with easily oxidizable materials and with the nucleic acids of DNA. Other free radicals are thought to degrade larger molecular units into smaller ones (46). There may also be an attack on the enzymes or precursors involved in the synthesis of DNA. It is likely that cancer may arise through alteration of DNA as a result of the action of endogenous free radicals.

Those who propose the free radical theory of aging point to its fundamental, microscopic nature and say proudly that all other theories are explainable within the framework of the free radical theory. Thus changes in the properties of connective tissue with age and decreasing heart function and senility of the nervous system reflect mutations in DNA or other changes wrought by the free radicals. We can now see aging of an organism as a unified process, according to the free radicalists (46).

Free radical inhibitors were tested on mice by adding the inhibitors to their daily diet as they grew from age two months to 20 months. Table XVIII shows the life extending effect com-

TABLE XVIII

EFFECT OF FREE RADICAL INHIBITORS ON
LIFESPAN OF MICE*

(MALE LAF₁ MICE, GROWING FROM AGE 2 MONTHS TO
20 MONTHS)

	% Survivors
Control	8.7
1.0 % 2-mercaptoethylamine-hydrochloride (2-MEA)	8.8
0.5 % butylated hydroxytoluene (BHT)	61.1
0.25 % 1,2 dihydro-6-ethoxy-2,2,4-trimethylquinoline (DETQ)	74.6
1.0 % ammonium diethyldithiocarbamate (DDC)	65.5
1.0 % sodium hypophosphate (NaHP)	28.8
1.0 % sodium bisulfite (NaBS)	17.0
0.5 % α-tocopheryl acetate (VE)	13.2
0.5 % VE + 0.5 % BHT	32.8
0.5 % VE + 1.0 % 2-MEA	6.3

*From Harman (4).

pared to a control group. From Table XVIII we see that BHT, DETQ and DDC dramatically increase the normal lifespan of mice, which raises questions about the efficacy of the chemicals in human experiments. We simply don't know whether a similar life extension effect can be obtained for humans since no experimental results have been published. So if aging is, at least in part, the result of free radical reactions produced in the course of our metabolic functions or by the interaction of oxygen with catalysts such as iron, copper and cobalt, then free radical scavengers would be expected to slow the aging process (8).

In another experiment mice were obtained shortly after weaning, divided into groups of about 30, and fed daily a powdered diet containing an antioxidant, free radical scavenger. The mice were weighed and counted every month and the data reported as shown in Table XIX.

TABLE XIX

SURVIVAL DATA FOR SOME MICE FED FREE
RADICAL SCAVENGERS*

Antioxidant	*Age at which 50% of the Mice were Dead*
cysteine hydrochloride, 1.0 %	10.5 months
2-MEA hydrochloride, 1.0 %	10.5 months
2,2-diaminediethyldisulfidedihydrochloride, 0.5%	10.6 months
control group	7.6 months
ascorbic acid (vitamin C), 2 %	7.6 months
2-mercaptoethanol, 0.5 %	7.6 months

*From Harman (46).

Continuing this experiment on Swiss male mice as well as AKR males and C3H female mice, pelleted food with antioxidants was used instead of powdered meal in the hope of achieving elevated concentrations of the antioxidants for longer periods of time. Table XX gives the results. Other researchers (7) were able to extend the lifespan of mice from 14.5 to 18.3 months with 2-MEA hydrochloride (1%). With cysteine hydrochloride (1%) and hydroxylamine hydrochloride (2%), the survival time was prolonged from 9.6 to 11.0 and 11.2 months respectively. Attempts

TABLE XX
SURVIVAL DATA FOR SPECIFIC STRAINS OF
MICE FED ANTIOXIDANTS*

Antioxidant	Age at which 50% of the Mice were Dead, months	
	AKR	C3H
Control	9.6	14.5
cysteine hydrochloride, 1 %	11.0	same as control
hydroxylamine hydrochloride, 2 %	11.2	15.5
2-MEA hydrochloride, 1 %	same as control	18.3
2-2 diaminediethyldisulfide, 1 %	toxic to mice	

(None of the antioxidants prolonged the lifespan of Swiss mice.)
*From Harman (46)

to prolong life by anti-radiation drugs and antioxidants have so far produced mixed results. Best results are claimed for immunosuppresent drugs (21).

Older persons with low blood levels of vitamin A and C have a higher mortality rate than do their cohorts with higher blood concentrations of the two vitamins. (Vitamins A and C are easily oxidized materials and hence act as antioxidants and free radical scavengers in the cells.) There is found in humans a decrease in the concentration of mercaptans with age, from 55 micromoles per 100 milliliters of serum at about age 30, to a corresponding level of 40 at age 80. There is also a similar loss of vitamin C with age (46). Thus we age faster as we get older, and this may be related to a continuous loss of antioxidant materials which apparently can stave off or moderate the aging process. Fact or fancy?

In another study on mice (47), 2-MEA and BHT were found to increase the mean lifespan of male mice, as shown in Figures 41 and 42.

In addition to the extension of lifespan, antioxidants are also reputed to be instrumental in decreasing lipofuscin accumulation, slowing blood vessel fibrosis and reducing tumor incidence in mice. So attractive is the idea of supplementing normal diets with antioxidants and extending life, that various formulations for humans such as those shown below are now being tested. The

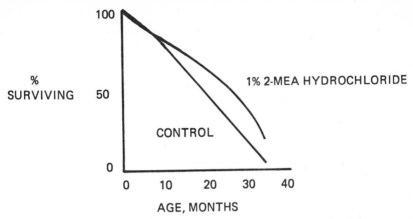

Figure 41.   Survival curve for LAF₁ male mice, showing the lifespan extension due to the addition of 1 percent 2-MEA hydrochloride in a commercial diet (from Harman [47]). The mean lifespan was increased, not the ultimate lifespan.

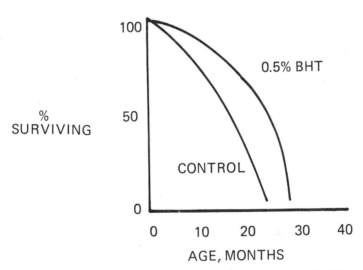

Figure 42.   Survival curve for LAF₁ male mice as a function of 0.5 percent BHT in a synthetic diet: casein; glucose; B vitamins; fat soluble vitamins in corn oil, salts, choline dihydrogen citrate, vitamins A and D, α-tocopherol, thiamin hydrochloride, riboflavin, pyridoxine hydrochloride, calcium pantothenate, folic acid, niamin, inositol, biotin, vitamin B-12, PABA, menadione (from Harman [47]).

diets are combinations of antioxidants, radiation-protecting drugs, and protein missynthesis resorters (48). (A protein missynthesis resorter is a chemical which is supposed to be able to diminish the deleterious effects of cross-linked DNA. It works by breaking down the poorly synthesized protein into its amino acid components, making them available again for metabolism [48].) The formulations come with a somber warning: the ingredients are

#1	#2
α - tocopherol	α - tocopherol
cysteine	cysteine
selenocystine	selenocystine
	BHT

to be taken in very definite prescribed ratios to prevent toxic effects from selenocystine, and it is suggested that self-experimentation would be highly dangerous. The inventors of these formulations also say that some combinations of the ingredients will not produce the desired synergistic effects, implying an additional warning against unauthorized experimentation.

The free radicalists estimate that with proper antioxidant therapy, we should be able to add five to ten years to the human lifespan. Radiation protection could add two to five years, and success with protein missynthesis resorters might contribute five to ten years of extended life. The three effects together, acting synergistically, have the potential for augmenting lifespan 30 to 40 years. Certain combinations of water-soluble and lipid-soluble antioxidants can stabilize cell membranes and protect other cell components against free radical attack, say the promoters of the free radical theory of aging. Sulfhydryls are supposed to be protectors against radiation damage as well as being free radical scavengers, peroxide decomposers, and repairers of already damaged cell material (48). Selenium (a very toxic substance) and some organic-selenium complexes help the body to assimilate vitamin E and are also free radical scavengers. Chemicals such as selenium, sulfhydryls and amino acid materials containing them, as well as folic acid, are thought to be useful as degraders of missynthesized proteins produced by faulty DNA. These ideas and hopes are as yet unverified and unfulfilled. The diet formulations have not been used to obtain significant published experimental data, so the speculation remains only a very enticing dream.

Attempts to extend life are also related to an interest in nutrition. Vitamin E deficiencies, in addition to generating an accelerated free radical attack, may also lead to a reduction in cell membrane stability. Vitamin C deficiencies could also lead to a decreased cell membrane stability but might additionally yield shrunken collagen which will diminish tissue permeability, giving some cell impairment. The nutrients most lacking in our average diet are the water-soluble vitamins (B-complex and C); vitamin E; sulfur-containing amino acids; and the minerals calcium, iron, manganese, zinc and selenium (49). Table XXI lists the important nutrients and their naturally occurring sources.

TABLE XXI

NATURAL SOURCES OF SOME IMPORTANT NUTRIENTS*

Selenium	tuna, herring, menhaden, anchovetta, brewers yeast, wheat germ, bran, broccoli, onions, cabbage, tomatoes
Sulfer-containing Amino Acids	eggs, cabbage, muscle meats
Vitamin E	wheat germ oil, leafy vegetables, eggs, muscle meats, fish, whole wheat, vegetable oils
B-complex Vitamins	brewers yeast, liver, sprouts, wheat germ
Vitamin C	citrus fruits, berries, sprouted seeds

*From Passwater and Welker (48)

In Rebuttal to the Free Radical Theory

There is wide disagreement on the efficacy of the various formulations for food supplements proposed by the free radicalists. One researcher, rebutting the claims, said (51),

Scientifically, there is litle data to support the claim that selenium-containing amino acids function as protein missynthesis resorters.

Incorporation of selenium into proteins has been demonstrated, but the resulting functional consequence has not been evaluated adequately. Butylated hydroxytoluene is commonly used in low amounts as a protective antioxidant for vitamin E; however toxic effects of the compound in higher doses have been demonstrated and its use in drug levels is certainly questionable. Antioxidants, sulfur compounds and steroids have been tested for their effects on lifespan, but their physiological and pathological effects on prolonged administration have not been tested adequately.

Another doubter wrote (52),

1. There is not a single published report of experimental evidence which demonstrates that aging is the result of, or even accompanied by, protein missynthesis. Coding errors have been reported to occur, but again there is not the slightest bit of evidence to suggest that such a phenomenon is age-dependent.

2. There is not a single published report of experimental evidence which demonstrates interference of age-dependent deterioration of physiological function following the administration of drugs.

So, not surprisingly, the evidence is still lacking in the search to confirm or deny the validity of the free radical theory of aging and the neutralization or moderation of the aging process by antioxidant and other chemical therapy.

THE CROSS-LINKING (COLLAGEN) THEORY OF AGING

Extracellular water diminishes with age, showing at the same time an increased concentration of sodium, calcium and chlorine ions. The volume occupied by the cells shrinks and so we shrink also (33). Human tendons appear fibrous and dried out in the aged. For developing humans, the body water content in bone is about 60 percent; for old bone it has depleted to about 10 percent (33). The water in bones is believed to be replaced by collagen and polysaccharides. Aged calcium appears to be tied to elastin; the pulmonary artery shows an age-related increase in calcium.

Collagen, which makes up about one-third of the total body protein, is present in and around blood vessels and the heart. The passage of material into and out of blood vessel walls is through collagen, and so it is apparent that the condition (permeability) of the collagen is critical for proper bodily functions. If our collagen becomes stiff and excessively cross-linked, this will limit fibril flexibility, the heart will not be able to constrict as well as it might, thus putting a strain on the heart. Large arteries become stiffened also. There is a diminished passage of gases, nutrients, metabolites, antibodies and toxins through the vessels. Hypertension can result, hypoxia (lack of oxygen) can occur in the cells — possibly causing them to become neoplastic — and cancer may result (33). Aged connective tissue is more easily invaded by tumors (33). But there are puzzling data which give rise to uncomfortable doubts about the relationship between collagen and tumors. It is known that the incidence of tumors does not increase steadily with age but seems to appear overwhelmingly only at advanced age (33). If the collagen theories are reasonable, tumors should appear at a steady rate from birth to death. Perhaps they do, but then the body is somehow able to neutralize them when we are young. Collagen is synthesized as soluble molecules that aggregate to form insoluble collagen fibrils. With age, we get more and more insoluble collagen fibrils (33). As long as the animal is growing, it apparently can synthesize young (soluble) collagen (33).

Researchers who study the aging process have always noted the similarities between aged human skin and tanned leather. Chemical tanning of leather is actually a cross-linking of cells which become bound to their neighbors — suggesting an analogy between this occurrence and that which occurs to the aging protein of the skin. Extending this cross-linking concept uniformly for all organs of the body, one can speculate on the possibility of serious, fatal harm being done to living systems as a result of cross-linking of large molecules in the body. Early in this century it was demonstrated that for large molecules, one cross-linkage for every 30,000 components is enough to drastically change the solubility and behavior of the molecule (49).

Within the living cell, DNA has a particular steric configuration; should some disruptive agent appear (such as free radicals), two or more DNA molecules may be tied together by cross-linking some of their components, seriously disturbing the effectiveness of the DNA. Many changes in function will result, particularly serious is the generation of missynthesized materials which cannot be acted upon normally by the body enzymes. Thus these "foreign" bodies may accumulate, crowding out other constituents, causing a decline in cell function. There could be molecular havoc produced by cross-linking, with the normal, precise arrangements of proteins and enzymes in the cells and membranes badly disrupted and their biological activities stymied. Collagen and elastin seem to manifest the effects of cross-linking most dramatically between ages 30 and 50 years in humans, caused by a "tanning" or formaldehyde-like chemical reaction (49, 33). Proponents of cross-linking say that aging is caused by monotonically increasing cross-linkages of protein and nucleic acid molecules, leading to progressive deterioration of chemical performance and eventual death of the organism.

Cross-linking can also take place between large molecules such as DNA and smaller, "cross-linker types," capable of reacting with two different large molecules and thereby forming a bridge between the large ones. This reduces the mobility of the linked molecules and leads to the formation of aggregates which have new diffusion properties as well as altered permeability and other essential characteristics (35). The damage to DNA is probably that of a cross-linking of two helices, making it impossible for one of the helices to act as a template in repairing the other (35).

The principal effect of radiation is thought to be a cross-linking one, mediated by the presence of free radicals. The other result of irradiation is a chain splitting effect, but it is thought now that the fragments which are produced from the fission are usually small enough to be excretable. Thus we see that cross-linking, radiation, and free radical concepts are intermingled. Perhaps the various theories of aging, though presented as separate entities, are in actuality all part of an overall scheme of aging which is not yet developed.

The human organism is pervaded by numerous cross-linking agents such as formaldehyde, acetaldehyde, glyoxal, glycoaldehyde, glyceraldehyde, pyruvaldehyde, croton aldehyde, malic acid, succinic acid, fumaric acid, quinones, orthoquinones, silicon, copper, aluminum, manganese, and oxidizing fats (35). Unsaturated fats, when oxidized, form some aldehydes, peroxides and free radicals which are cross-linkers. With all of these materials present in the cells in relative abundance, it is frequently asked why the aging process in humans does not proceed rapidly to its conclusion in a matter of months rather than decades. The answer seems to be that there is a steady breakdown of mildly cross-linked protein molecules into simpler constituents and a resynthesis of these components into viable, non-cross-linked materials. Hence there is a rapid turnover of protein, a reasonable balance of errors is struck, and the aging process then proceeds at a more moderate pace.

Many investigators have shown that collagen becomes cross-linked (35) and is increasingly polymerized during maturation. Some interesting experiments on human skin showed that aged collagen has more cross-links than young collagen and that lysine-derived cross-links form an important structural component of aged elastin (35). Other research stresses the effect of tyrosine as a starting point in collagen cross-linking, and it was found that free tyrosine (not tied up in the cross-linked molecules) decreases with age in collagen. These observations lend credance to speculation that the oxidation of tyrosine leads to a quinone-like structure which binds to adjacent materials and causes cross-linking. These quinone-like materials have also been isolated from aged heart muscles, apparently strongly linked to the heart material.

The lens of the eyes loses its ability to form vitamin C with age (35). Such a vitamin C deficient animal is prone to cataracts if a derivative of quinone (quinoniminecarboxylic acid) is injected intraperitoneally, which leads to some speculation that old age is related to these quinone-like substances and a loss of some essential chemical like vitamin C. Animals can be induced to grow cataracts by treatments involving naphthalene, dinitrophenol and galactose. From the urine of these animals quinone derivatives can be extracted. So again we may be going around in circles, but there does seem to be some connection between collagen, aging, DNA, vitamin C, quinone and cataracts, though the connections are not yet ordered. The proponents of cross-linking as a theory of aging also find support in the experimental results which show an accumulation with age of nitrogenous insoluble material such as lipofuscin in many organs and tissue (35).

The character of the cross-linked material apparently varies from organ to organ, depending on the animal specie, nutritional factors, and other more indefinite things. With age, humans seem to concentrate metallic materials in arteries; analysis of the human aorta shows evidence of metallic oxides in the cross-linked tissue. Other locations show no metal concentrations. With over-feeding, it is suspected that body metabolism cannot readily oxidize the foods to the usual water and carbon dioxide, but also forms intermediate products of metabolism. Some of these intermediates are powerful cross-linkers and could accelerate the aging process. This is consistent with experimental evidence which indicates that obese or very well nourished persons have shorter lifespans than underfed, healthy individuals (35).

The cross-linking (collagen) believers propose that their theory of aging allows for the progressive reduction with age of the ability of hormones, enzymes and other essential materials to diffuse into and out of their active sites. Thus the life process slows down say the cross-linkers. Transmission speeds of nerve impulses are slowed down, among other things; and the living, dynamic system becomes progressively sluggish. Cross-linking agents are so many and so varied that avoidance of the agents in the diet or environment is impossible.

If the effect of overeating is to produce a larger than normal concentration of deleterious free radicals and cross-linking agents, then it is argued that many small meals would be preferable to a few large ones. (It has been shown that intermittent fasting periods are beneficial for maximum lifespan attainment [35].) Ingesting sufficient vitamin E and and other antioxidants would be expected to be effective in neutralizing those cross-linkers which result from the oxidative process in the body (such as aldehydes and peroxides from unsaturated fatty acids [35].)

Cross-linkers in the cell membranes could be minimized by treatment with tocopherols (vitamin E) and other antioxidants of this genre. Researchers of the cross-linking persuasion also promote the use of dietary means for supplying a surplus of scavengers for the cross-linked molecules. Now if the scavengers do their job, and if the breakdown products are easily excretable from the body, then the progressive effect of cross-linking and aging can be moderated (35).

The cross-link theorists also suspect that bad things come from metals such as copper, cadmium, lead, aluminum and silicon, which are known to increase in concentration with age and accumulate in "aged" organs. If these metals could be removed from the body by use of chelating agents, would cross-links be reduced and hence would the aging process also decline? Some researchers have shown that the lifespan of sea urchin spermatozoa are multiplied several times if these metals are removed by chelating agents (35). Some think this procedure could be successful in rejuvenating the circulatory system in humans. Other treatments for the tendons (where cross-linking does not involve metals) could use ethylene diamine tetra acetic acid (EDTA), sulfhydryl materials, and other agents to neutralize the cross-linked structure. It is suggested that it might be beneficial in the aged to use zinc salts to displace cadmium. All these treatments are speculative and have not yet been tried. They are also presumed to be ineffective against quinone cross-linkages. Nitrites may interfere with the maturation of collagen and elastin, and so it is natural that these chemicals have been used in attempts to inhibit aging — but with no success (33).

What we are looking for is a way of reversing the aging process, whereby we would break down the excessively cross-linked materials in the cells and make the cellular space available for other "normal" anabolic processes which could rejuvenate the cells. This can apparently be done for collagen in the uterus of rats, where cross-linked collagen can be made to be resorbed. If it is possible for one type of protein, can we do it for other proteins (35)?

Some researchers suggest that we ought to seek these wondrous cross-link breakers from enzymes of soil bacteria (35), led in this direction apparently by the knowledge that some soil bacteria do break down fossil protein and thus there must be some enzymes which make this possible. One of these enzymes might be our magic bullet. If the enzyme also attacked other proteins, this wouldn't be too objectionable as long as the normal anabolic processes of the body replaced the healthy protein which was removed. There is some evidence that proteolytic enzymes (which break down proteins into fragments) used in the treatment of experimentally induced hematomas can actually reach the cells of the liver and kidney, even if the enzymes are given orally (35). Does this suggest an experimental approach? Some investigators say that old cross-linked collagen in wounds can be broken down (35). So the search goes on for an effective proteinase which will have an affinity for cross-linked material.

THE SOMATIC MUTATION (AND IMMUNOLOGIC) THEORY OF AGING

The diameter of the smallest microorganism capable of independent reproduction is about 5,000 Angstroms. Viruses are on the order of 250 Angstroms, but they are unable to metabolize, or grow, or undergo binary fission, for they are intracellular parasites and require host cells to provide metabolic processes. (A virion is an infectious virus particle [37].) Every cell has DNA and RNA; a virion has only one or the other.)

X-rays, ultraviolet rays, nitrogen mustard, organic peroxides and nitrous acid are mutagenic. When bacteria or bacteriophage are exposed to nitrous acid, we get mutants. It is believed that nitrous acid deaminates (removes NH_2 groups from) nucleic acid materials. Since nucleic acids promulgate hereditary properties and the synthesis of proteins and enzymes, this damage is critical (37).

Young and old animals exposed to low oxygen concentrations for long periods respond differently. The mitochondria of old rats are more severely affected by this stress, becoming swollen and fragmented. These old mitochondria are more sensitive to freezing and thawing cycles among other weaknesses (33). Growing and active animals generally have tissue showing higher metabolic rates and higher concentrations of enzymes than their older cohorts, as shown in Figure 43.

There is an increase in the number of aneuploid lymphocytes in aged human females (33). In almost all cases of known intracellular breakdown due to aging, there is an increased concentration of lysosomes which hydrolyze the organic material (such as skeletal muscle). But are the lysosomes simply scavengers for debris or is there something "sinister" in their presence?

The somatic mutation theory states that (1) spontaneous mutations of somatic cells, propagated by cell divisions, cause the formation of inferior cells by changes in nucleic acid templates and (2) mutated cells form more often in old individuals (35). Since most mutations are harmful, the living system, with age, becomes less efficient and eventually is unable to survive. Those who promote the mutation theory further say that the mutated cells stimulate immunologic reactions within the organism which eventually destroy or weaken the host functions and we die (50). (The relationship between the somatic mutation theory, the cross-link theory, and the free radical theory is apparent; sooner or later the proponents of each must recognize that they are probably dealing with only one fundamental concept — though they hold onto different parts of it.)

Somatic mutationists proclaim further their belief that spon-

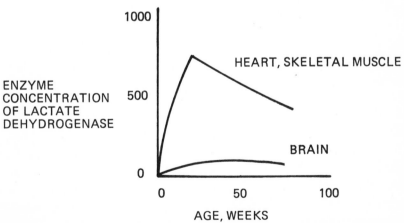

Figure 43.   Change in concentration of one enzyme with age for rats (from Kohn [33], p. 54).

taneous mutations build up in both dividing and non-dividing cells. Non-dividing cells such as aging red blood cells have increasing numbers of abnormal cohorts. In some experiments, liver cells with lesions in the genome were allowed to regenerate; and when cell division had occurred, the aberrations were observed to have been transferred to the new cells. (The experiment is done by inserting carbon tetrachloride subcutaneously, destroying most of the liver.) Another chemical mutagenic agent, nitrogen mustard, is known to break chromosomes in bone marrow and intestinal cells, where cells are rapidly dividing. On the other hand, the nitrogen mustard causes no unusual aberrations in the normally non-dividing cells of the liver. Thus nitrogen mustard should not affect lifespan statistics in the same way as other mutants. Low level x-rays or gamma radiation over a period of months is only about one-fourth as effective in shortening lifespan as a single dose at a high level (31). But long-term, low level neutron irradiation is just as effective in shortening lifespan as a large, single dose, as measured by chromosome damage.

Discussion of mutations in cells leads naturally to DNA which constitutes the chromosomes of the nucleus. A single DNA molecule is responsible for each function in the cell, such as replication during cell division (through RNA messenger units which the DNA produces). RNA diffuses out into the cell cytoplasm where it synthesizes a particular enzyme. Mutagenic agents are thought to damage the DNA and eventually kill or alter the cell. The most difficult task for a mitotic (dividing) cell is the division process, since the cell needs all of its DNA for this operation. Irradiated cells appear normal until cell division occurs when they may die or give bizarre daughter cells.

In living and dying, chemicals within the cells are synthesized, degraded and rejected or resorbed. Some materials, like DNA, once synthesized, do age but are not readily degraded. On the other hand, RNA apparently can disappear, having a half-life of one hour or less. More RNA must be continuously generated. Organelles have a rapid turnover in the cells. Liver mitochondria have a half-life on the order of ten days. Some microsomal protein has a half-life of about one day. Somehow, the enzymes which degrade or break down these age-altered molecules are able to recognize the difference between young and old. They selectively degrade the old, which are replaced by a young, newly synthesized population (33). Organelles age with associated protein denaturation, loss of morphological integrity, and fragmentation and vacuolization. Denatured protein is more easily broken down by enzymes which are specialists in this work (33). There is also fragmentation in the Golgi apparatus with age.

In the body, some cells undergo regular divisions (skin) or rarely divide (liver) or never divide (brain). It is thought that mutations in cells which undergo regular divisions cause little permanent damage to the organ involved, since the mutated cells will die or lose out in the competition with other cells (31). Some researchers think that organs which have non-dividing cells should ultimately be responsible for the aging process and senescence. They cite the example of blood forming organs (with dividing cells) which function far into old age whereas muscles (non-dividing cells) show the first signs of aging. However, non-dividing cells can apparently function nearly normally for long periods with damaged chromosomes — using up the previously formed, normal RNA of the cytoplasm. Mammalian dividing cells can frequently continue three to five divisions after a moderate dose of radiation before the daughter cells die or become bizarre; mammalian non-dividing cells (red blood cells) function normally for a long time without a nucleus (31).

The somatic mutationists proclaim that the genetic structure of the cells, in the chromosomes, carry the function and instructions; when the chromosomes are damaged, there could be a synthesis of wrong proteins. The errors will be propogated by the daughter cells. The mutations will accumulate until a significant portion of the organism is "aged" and eventually dies (53). X-rays which cause mutations are known to shorten life expectancy in proportion to the dosage. The victim assumes the characteristics of a naturally aged person so one concludes that there is an aging destructiveness to radiation. But radiation results are not intrinsically germane to the somatic mutation hypothesis, since the radiation is an external stress imposed and

thus any support these data provide is beneficial only by in-
ference.

But how do you measure a mutation? For some mammalian
cells such as liver cells, which seldom undergo division in the
adult organism, it is possible to induce cell division by a partial
hepatectomy. After about 72 hours, samples of the cells are collected and some cell division can be seen (53). If we take the
liver cells as representative of the changes wrought in the chromosomes of somatic cells, an indication of the total mutation rate
can be obtained. By this technique, some conclusions can be
drawn, as listed below (35):

1. Chromosome aberration increases steadily with age. In old
mice, rats and dogs, 75 percent of all liver cells contain abnormal
chromosomes.

2. Radiation increases the number of mutations markedly
and in proportion to the dosage.

3. Long-lived mice develop mutations at a slower rate than
the short-lived ones.

4. Dogs develop aberrations in their chromosomes at a
slower rate than mice and age at a correspondingly slower rate.

Thus there is evidence for support of the idea that mutations
occur more frequently in short-lived animals than in long-lived
ones and that this is the "reason" for differences in lifespan. But
we haven't dealt with the question — the more significant aspect
of our search for the truth — of why the mutations occur. There
is no answer to this question from the somatic mutationists.

Further support for somatic mutation as a theory of aging
rests on observations of the growth of one type of tumor in
women. Tissue from these tumors have only one type of enzyme
present on the X chromosome (type A or B of glucose-6-phosphate
dehydrogenase). Normally it would be expected that the cells
would have equal amounts of both A and B enzymes. The fact
that there is only one type of enzyme present is taken as a strong
indication that mutations must have occurred, resulting in tumor
development which is usually associated with the aging process
(53). Other investigators think they have demonstrated that
atherosclerosis is caused by mutations in the arterial endothelial

cells. In related work, it has been shown that radiation seems to induce atherosclerosis in some pigeons (53). Mutagenic chemicals are also now known to cause cancer. Some investigators suggest that autoimmune reactions and diseases, start with a mutation and show this by radiation experiments (53).

But not everyone agrees that the somatic mutation theory is the most probable or the only theory which can explain the process of aging. The dissenters say that too many other factors are known to be involved. Even in cancers induced by radiation, some believe that it is not the mutated cells which finally form the cancer (53). They cite the evidence that we can increase the incidence of mutations in an organism, yet tumor frequency is not proportional to the number of mutations; and the diminishment of life expectancy does not keep pace either (53). Also there is some time lag between the production of mutations and the tumors which are generated, which seems unreasonable to some researchers, particularly unreasonable when in some cases this latent period is 40 years. We also have identified "precancerous tissue" which beclouds the logical connection between mutations, aging and cancer. There may be thousands of cells in a tissue sample, and skeptics find it difficult to allow that a cancerous mutation has occurred simultaneously in all of these cells. Further, it has been found that some strains of mice which die of leukemia at about 10 months of age do not develop chromosome aberrations in their liver cells any faster than non-leukemic strains (53).

So there are plenty of doubters for every proponent of the somatic mutation theory of aging. After x-radiation, the number of chromosome aberrations returns to the control level of the untreated animals, so that in some cases, while the increased death rate is being felt, the chromosome aberration count is normal. This seems to point to some inconsistency in the logic employed by the somatic mutationists.

For those who are tied to the logical connection between radiation experiments and verification of their hypotheses, some critics have pointedly warned that the conclusions are subject to serious challenge. They point out that at doses below 200 roentgens, cell damage in mammals is in the chromosomes; but not all fixed post-mitotic cells are equally sensitive to the radiation. Thus there is experimental evidence which shows that irradiated flies live longer than their cohorts under some circumstances, as shown in Figure 44. It is thought that this increased longevity may be due to a difference in effects resulting from low versus high doses of radiation. In organisms where the cellular makeup is fixed and there is no cell division, radiation does shorten lifespan but only at dosages one or two orders of magnitude greater than that which shortens the life of rodents (54). There are also signs that clonally dividing mammalian cells can alter the effect on them of low-dose radiation (54). Thus we have some apparent contradictions and more data is needed in order to find the basic underlying unity of concept − if it exists. The two schools of thought − somatic mutation and autoimmunity − have now merged their ideas and present a unified platform of principles (54):

1. Somatic mutation alters tissue cells, which eventually impairs the vigor of the tissue.

2. As a result of somatic mutations, there is generated some

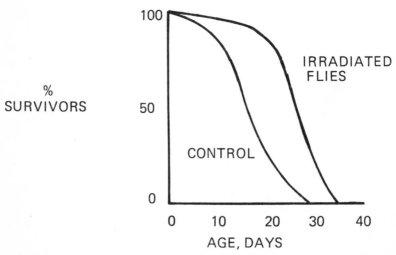

Figure 44.   Increase in lifespan of drosophila flies with a radiation dose of 4300 roentgens (from Strehler [42], p. 194).

new cells which are different from the originals. These altered cells generate or excite the immunity (antibody) mechanism in the organism and we have autoimmune reactions.

3. There is suggested, therefore, a connection between the aging process, mutations and autoimmunity.

If mutations were limiting the length of life, one would expect diploid organisms to live longer than haploids, since diploids have a double set of chromosomes and thus a reserve set in case of a non-lethal mutation. However diploid cells do not necessarily live longer than haploids, casting some doubt on the somatic mutation theory of aging (35). In some experiments, rats were fed three mutagenic agents, two of which were known cross-linkers. If aging were due only to somatic mutations, all three mutagens should cause similar life-shortening effects. However only the cross-linkers showed life shortening effects similar to natural aging, which gave more support to the doubters of the somatic theory (35). In some animal experiments on irradiated haploid and diploid cells, there was no difference in lifespan shortening. But it was found that haploid males are more susceptible to radiation than are diploid males. So there is more confusion about somatic mutation since it may not be that the number of sets of chromosomes is a factor in natural aging (42).

Thus mutation in the genes may lead to the generation of incorrect messengers which yield products exhibiting immunological incompatibility. The mutated cell misidentifies itself to its cellular neighbors, evoking reprisals against the mutation — and perhaps against its normal neighbors (54). But doubters point to arthritis versus age data for men and women and disagree. Women suffer from this disease more than men, in a ratio of approximately two to one. If arthritis is brought on by an autoimmune reaction from a mutated cell or antibody, then women should have twice as many antibody producing clones than men. With more antibodies, women should have a lower incidence of infectious diseases than men, which they do. But with more antibody producing clones in women than men, we must conclude from the autoimmunity theory of aging that women should age about twice as fast as men — which they do not. Women actually age a bit more slowly, and we have arrived at a wrong conclusion based on "correct" logic (54). So once again we find the arguments both for and against an attractive theory of aging to be persuasive.

In relating aging to immune reactions, some investigators suggest that we have, due to mutations, a breakdown in the mechanism which normally prevents lymphocytes from producing antibodies antagonistic towards its own body material (54). With age, the mutated lymphocytes may produce antibodies which attack the host organism. This line of reasoning places the mutational process in the antibody producing cells rather than in the tissue cells and avoids the illogic of somatic mutation theory which says that aging is caused by a cell by cell mutation procedure — a relatively slow process. Radiation may raise the somatic mutation rate, but that alone would not seem able to account for the aging process. Thus we conclude that something else is at work in aging, in addition to somatic mutation: a suspicion that antibodies may be involved (54). An error in the antibody producer needs only one mutation followed by rapid clonal multiplication and we have the possibilities of the extensive, progressive damage we recognize as old age.

CHAPTER 7

SOME FAVORED MACROSCOPIC THEORIES OF AGING

MACROSCOPIC THEORIES OF AGING are those which deal with the process on the organism level, not on the microscopic, cellular level. Macroscopic theories do not get to the heart of the matter, do not consider "why it happens," but rather they are concerned mostly with attempts to describe the results of aging. Thus no matter how correct the macroscopic theory may be, the mechanism for aging can only be discovered by induction. Nevertheless the macroscopic approach is useful, for it is essential that we build on experimental observations of the whole animal. Ideally, the microscopic and macroscopic approaches converge, as the ultimate truth is approached and seeming inconsistencies diminish.

WEAR AND TEAR (RATE OF LIVING) THEORY OF AGING

Food fuels the body as gasoline energizes the automobile. Restrict the food intake and you slow the rate of living and diminish wear and tear on the organism. The life cycle of invertebrates is lengthened by giving less food than that which produces maximum growth and development (11). In old physiology texts as early as 1881 there is a reference to the dehydration of rotifers as a means of lengthening life (15). Larvae and adults of species which show continuous cell multiplication respond to moderate dietary restrictions by lengthening lifespan. Exceptions are animals which must draw on stored reserves in order to survive or those with a fixed number of cells and a need to replenish their reserves.

The lifespan of rats can be prolonged by restricting their growth by dietary means. After the restricted diet was replaced with a more normal diet, the survivors of these experiments resumed growth and lived longer than the control group. The effect seemed more dramatic in males. Similar results were found for mice and other rodents (11, 25). The basal metabolism of these rats on restricted diets were intermediate between the normal young and normal adults suggesting a "younger" condition. (An interesting question arises from these studies on rate of growth and ultimate lifespan: will the well-fed children in affluent countries achieve puberty sooner than less privileged children elsewhere and will this result in shorter lifespans?)

Extending life by partial starvation is best done for very young rats: the normal lifespan of the white rat (500 to 700 days) can be extended to 1000 to 1400 days by keeping young rats underfed (15, 25). Tumors normally transplantable from one rat to another will not take in underfed rats (15). When the life of an animal is extended by retarding its growth by dietary means, some parts of the body still appear to age at the regular rate. Bones become old and fragile normally, although they will grow after the diet is normalized. Hair and skin manage to retain their youthful looks in the retarded animals; diseases come more slowly. But when the skin is cut, it seems tough — like older skin (16). Thus the bones of the retarded white rat at 1400 days are fragile. Their eyes fail at the same rate as the normal rats (16). The retarded animals never attain normal adult size though they live longer than the control group (16). Optimal growth is not necessarily conducive to greatest longevity.

If an organ such as the kidney is severely damaged, it will not completely recover and hence becomes more vulnerable to disease and trauma. Damage in mammalian tissue usually leads to fibrosis which diminishes its function. In our lifetime, as we suffer these upsets and accidents, we wear out (53). In some cases, increases in stress (disease) decrease life expectancy (31). Radiation is a non-specific stress; mutagenic agents are another type of stress vector. For example, mice subjected to nitrogen mustard (a mutagen) and typhoid toxin died at an accelerated rate. But the survivors lived as long as the control group (31). The same experimental procedure, but with x-rays as the stress agent, showed that the survivors had a reduced lifespan. A tentative conclusion we can reach is that the mice able to survive the nitrogen mustard treatment, the hardy ones, are essentially unchanged. This type of stress apparently is not lasting (31). So in some cases wear and tear does cause aging but there seem to be apparent exceptions, such as shown by the nitrogen mustard experiments (53).

The rate of living theorists say simply that our body has a programmed amount of energy, entropy or other property which is used up as a function of life and living. When we deplete this life substance, if the residual level drops to some critical amount, or if the rate at which we consume it drops to some sensitive mark, then we are sufficiently weakened and we die. (The engine runs out of gas.) This model has some obvious validity for those insects which have no mouths in their adult forms and thus are limited in energy and lifespan to the stores of food they accumulate during their larval state (42).

In trying to find a "rate of living" explanation for the aging process, interest naturally turns to basal metabolism, which is the heat given off by the whole organism under controlled, resting conditions. We have data which shows that the maximum rate of basal metabolism occurs during the first decade of life, falls off rapidly during the second decade and decreases gradually thereafter (40). Basal metabolism is related to oxygen consumption, and some investigators measure the oxygen used by the living system and express it in terms of basal heat given off. Figure 45 shows basal metabolism in terms of oxygen consumption for the thalamus, and we see that the maximum rate occurs early in life and then decreases thereafter. Is the lowered rate due to a loss of cells or a lessening of the actual usage of oxygen? It is thought now that for the thalamus, and also for the brain as a whole, the decrease in oxygen consumption we see is due to a loss of cells. However, in rabbits there seems to be an anomaly: by two and one-half years of age, there is already a reduction of about 20 percent in oxygen consumption of the brain even though the weight of the brain is still increasing (40).

We know that the greater the metabolic rate, the shorter

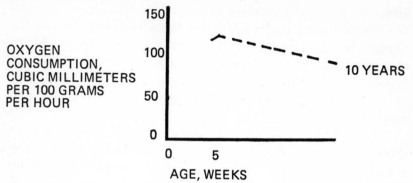

OXYGEN
CONSUMPTION,
CUBIC MILLIMETERS
PER 100 GRAMS
PER HOUR

Figure 45. Oxygen consumption with age for the thalamus (from Birren [40], p. 205).

the lifespan — man and mouse each expend a total of about 700 calories per gram of body weight in their lifetimes, but the mouse uses its energy about 30 times faster than man and has a lifespan which is about one-thirtieth that of man (50). There are many difficulties with these ideas, such as the evidence that for humans, exercise may actually prolong life (53). But there are counter arguments, and one cannot blithely dismiss the rate of living theory. There is a significant correlation between lifespan and basal metabolism which leads to some fascinating speculation about the "proper" way to measure age.

THE GOMPERTZ SURVIVAL EQUATION

We define a mortality rate, R_m, which is related to the instantaneous death rate divided by the population size,

where
$$R_m = -\frac{dn}{dt} \Big/ n$$

R_m = mortality rate

$\frac{dn}{dt}$ = death rate

n = population size

By curve-fitting survival data, we can derive (30)

$$\frac{N}{N_o} = e^{\left(\frac{R_o}{\alpha}\right)} \ (e^{\alpha t} - 1)$$

and

$$R_m = R_o \, e^{\alpha t} \; (\text{Gompertz equation})$$

where   N = number of deaths at time, t
   N_o = initial population size
   R_o = initial mortality rate
   α = a constant
   t = age

Thus nothing new is discovered here. We have expressed mathematically what is already known: as we age, the number of survivors diminishes and approaches zero in a manner described by the equations.

LOSS OF FUNCTION CORRELATIONS (30)

We know that basal metabolism and breathing capacity are lost as shown in Figure 46 and that nerve conduction velocity is down from 100 percent to 90 percent; cell water content goes from 100 percent to 80 percent; and the cardiac index decreases from 100 percent to 60 percent in aging from 30 to 90 years. There are a number of empirical correlations which have been published, attempting to organize this knowledge.

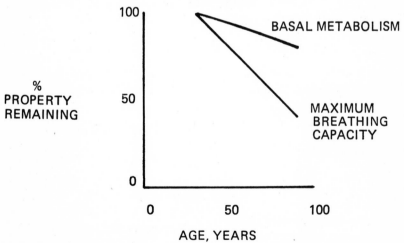

Figure 46. Loss of function data with age for humans (from Mildvan and Strehler [30]).

Brody-Failla (30)

$$\frac{dV}{dt} = -\alpha V \text{ or } V = V_o\, e^{-\alpha t}$$

where V = vitality (mortality, R_m, is inversely proportional to vitality, V)

    V_o = initial vitality

    t = age

From this we can get the Gompertz relationship

$$R_m = R_o\, e^{\alpha t}$$

where R_m = the mortality rate at time, t

    R_o = initial mortality rate

    α = a constant

    t = age

By matching these equations with survival data, we can infer that at age 80 we should have remaining only 1/300 of our vitality, which is not generally true. So there is significant criticism of even this simple, macroscopic, empirical approach.

Simm-Jones (30)

This approach hypothesizes that

$$V = V_o - C\,D$$

where V = vitality at time, t

    V_o = initial vitality

    C = a constant

    D = accumulated damage from disease and age

It is assumed that

$$\frac{dD}{dt} = \alpha D$$

where α = a constant

Combining these equations leads to

$$V = V_o - C\,D_o\, e^{\alpha t}$$

where D_o = initial damage suffered by the organism
This gives

$$R_m = k \, D = R_o \, e^{\alpha t} \text{ (the Gompertz relationship)}$$

where R_m = mortality rate (proportional to the damage, D)
$\quad$ k = a constant

Sacher (30)

There is a linear decay of physiologic states. Death occurs when a displacement of the physiologic state extends below a certain limiting value. This approach hypothesizes that the probability of dying increases with age. These ideas lead to

$$R_m = \frac{g}{\sigma} \, \lambda \, \left(\frac{2}{\pi} \right)^{1/2} \, e^{-\frac{\lambda^2}{2\sigma^2}}$$

where R_m = mortality rate
$\quad$ g,σ = constants
$\quad$ λ = M $-$ L
$\quad$ L = lower limit of the physiological state before death
$\qquad$ (a constant)
$\quad$ M = mean value of the physiological state

This equation and the hypotheses invoked can also lead to the Gompertz equation.

Strehler-Mildvan (30)

An organism is composed of subsystems which are displaced (and damaged) by internal stresses. We need energy to restore these subsystems to their original conditions. Vitality is the maximum rate of energy supply which is available for restoration of the original conditions. The frequency of encountering damaging stresses increases as the energy available for restoration decreases. The rate of death is proportional to the frequency of stresses which are beyond the ability of the subsystems to restore the initial conditions. From these ideas, we write some equations,

$$R_m = CX$$

where R_m = rate of death (mortality rate)

  X = frequency of killing stresses

  C = a constant

We can also get

$$R_m = k\,e^{-\dfrac{\Delta H}{RT}}$$

where k = a constant

  ΔH = size of energy fluctuations just sufficient to kill (vitality)

  RT = average size of energy fluctuations encountered

Using the Gompertz form

$$R_m = R_o\,e^{\alpha t},$$

we can ultimately get

$$\Delta H = \Delta H_o\,(1 - Bt)$$

where ΔH_o = initial size of energy fluctuations just sufficient to kill (initial vitality)

$$B = \frac{\alpha}{\ln K/R_o}$$

  α, K = constants

  R_o = initial mortality

Figure 47 shows how vitality should diminish with age for the four "theories" described above.

DIFFUSION THEORY

This theory hypothesizes that the accumulation of cross-linked molecules in cells is a diffusion-controlled phenomenon. This accumulation is expressed as (55):

$$\frac{dN}{dt} = \textit{(production rate)—(leakage out of the cell)—(break-down of cross-linkages)}$$

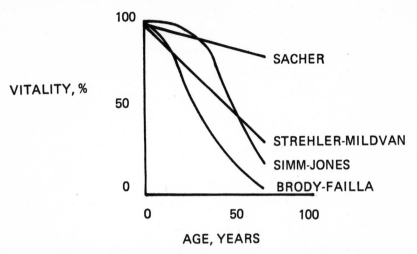

Figure 47. Loss of vitality predicted from some macroscopic theories (from Mildvan and Strehler [30]).

where N = the number of cross-linked molecules in a cell
 t = time

(production rate) $= P \left(1 - \dfrac{N}{N_m}\right)$

P = a constant for a particular type of molecule
N_m = maximum number of molecules which can be accumulated in a cell

(leakage out of the cell) $= - D \nabla^2 N =$ diffusion loss

D = diffusion coefficient
∇^2 = mathematical symbol

(breakdown of cross-linkages) $= \left(\dfrac{1}{g}\dfrac{dg}{dt}\right) N$

g = fraction of the mass of the body which can be classified as being in the adult stage

The transport of the molecules through the cell walls is given by

$$- D \frac{dn}{dr} = h (N - N_e)$$

where h   = cell wall permeability
    r   = radial distance in the spherical cell
    N_e = number of molecules outside the cell

All of these equations can be solved together, and the resulting solution predicts changes in macroscopic properties such as the change in strength of rat collagen (based on the hypothesis that the diffusion of cross-linked collagen out of the cells affects the extensibility of rat tendons).

These equations were also applied to the accumulation of age pigments (lipofuscin) in nerve and heart tissue. Figure 48 shows some of the results. This theory and its equations fit the experimental data as long as many unevaluated parameters are introduced into the equations. This curve-fitting technique is valuable in the sense that we use the data to determine the parameters. No essential truth can be uncovered about the aging mechanics, only that it may be described grossly.

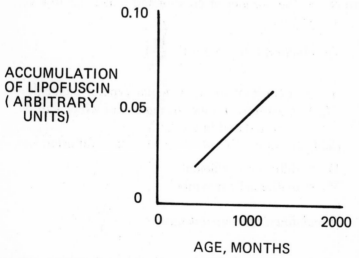

Figure 48.   Accumulation of lipofuscin with age for humans (from Carpenter [55]).

CHAPTER 8

BODY TEMPERATURE, BASAL METABOLISM AND AGING

EFFECT OF TEMPERATURE ON OXYGEN CONSUMPTION

THE FIRES OF LIFE BURN STEADILY and remarkably under control. Your body temperature is 98.6 degrees Fahrenheit or very close to it when all is well inside. Deviate ever so slightly in either direction and trouble is brewing.

One measure of body heat is the rectal temperature. Early risers have higher rectal temperatures in the morning (38), which seems to imply that their "engines" are warming up in anticipation of activity. And do you awaken because of the increased internal energy production? But is the rectal temperature the significant measure of body heat, for we know that skin temperature also varies with activity and ambient conditions. Recognizing this ambiguity, some researchers have defined a mean body temperature which is a combination of rectal and skin temperature (38)

$$T_B = 0.65\,T_R + 0.35\,T_S$$

where

T_B = mean body temperature, °C
T_R = rectal temperature, °C
T_S = mean surface temperature, °C

So now you must measure the temperature of various surfaces of the body, calculate the surface area, and come up with some sort of mean value. Table XXII shows these data, and it is apparent that this mean body temperature is not an easily accessible number.

TABLE XXII

SKIN TEMPERATURE, SURFACE AREA AND BASAL HEAT GENERATION
FOR VARIOUS REGIONS OF THE HUMAN BODY*

Region	Area m^2	Basal Temp. °C	Heat Loss $\frac{kcal}{hr}$	$\frac{kcal}{m^2.hr}$
Head	0.20	34.6	4.0	20.0
Chest	0.17	34.6	8.2	48.3
Abdomen	0.12	34.6	4.5	37.5
Back	0.23	34.6	12.4	53.9
Buttocks	0.18	34.6	8.3	46.2
Thighs	0.33	33.0	12.0	36.0
Calves	0.20	30.8	14.6	73.0
Feet	0.12	28.6	10.0	83.3
Arms	0.10	33.0	8.4	84.0
Forearms	0.08	30.8	8.6	107.5
Hands	0.07	28.6	16.0	228.6
Total body	1.80	33.0 (mean)	107.0	59.4

*From Burton and Collier (58)

There are a number of experimental correlations of skin surface area with other physical parameters which help translate something more easily measured into the more esoteric skin surface area (38). For example

$$S = 0.1 \, W^{2/3}$$

where

S = surface area, m^2

W = weight, kg

or

$$S = 71.84 \, H^{0.725} W^{0.425}$$

where

H = height, cm

There is even a relationship between body weight and pulse rate

$$P = 186 \, W^{-1/4}$$

where

P = pulse rate (beats/minute) for elephants, horses, cattle, sheep, rabbits

Homeotherms are animals such as mammals which maintain a constant temperature under normal living conditions. On the other hand, poikilotherms are the living things (such as fish) who assume the temperature of the environment. And there is another group, including hedgehogs and marmots who are homeothermic during warm or moderate temperatures but in winter they hibernate and cool off (38). Most birds and mammals regulate their oxygen consumption and body temperature within closely defined limits. Some species reduce body temperature and oxygen consumption and remain in a torpor for the winter (hibernators) or the summer (estivators) (26). In torpor, body heat generation (basal metabolism) depends crucially upon the ambient temperature. Some birds and mammals fail to emerge from torpor when the condition is entered below a certain temperature (26).

The body temperature of a human baby drops precipitously immediately after birth as if the newborn system is adjusting its thermostatic control to the new environment. At birth, full-term infants can increase their metabolic heat rates by about 100 percent in response to cold, which is a remarkable response that is unmatched thereafter. Apparently there is some sort of physiologic set-point associated with this heat control mechanism, for we can show that oxygen consumption (and heat production) rises when the ambient temperature is lowered below some critical temperature, as shown in Figure 49. If the ambient temperature is then returned to this critical temperature, oxygen consumption and heat production resume their characteristic levels (17). Apparently this critical temperature decreases with age; some data shows that it falls from 36°C to 32°C by the first week of life (17). It is believed that we all have a critical, set-point temperature and that our response to a cold environment is similar to the curves shown in Figure 49. Thus it should be possible to warm up (to increase the basal metabolic rate) by cooling a sensitive part of the body below its critical temperature.

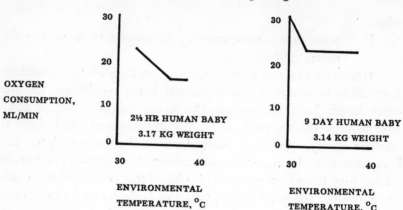

Figure 49. Oxygen consumption versus environmental temperature for human babies at two ages (from Hill and Rahimtulla [17]).

Various animals have different critical set-point temperatures as shown in Figure 50. The trends are similar for rabbits, chickens and mice but the critical temperatures are different. We see from Figures 50 and 51 (for rats and frogs) that subjecting these animals to ambient temperatures above or below the set-point raises the basal heat production.

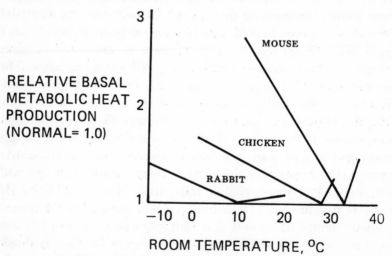

Figure 50. Basal metabolism versus room temperature for rabbits, chickens and mice (from Brody [57]).

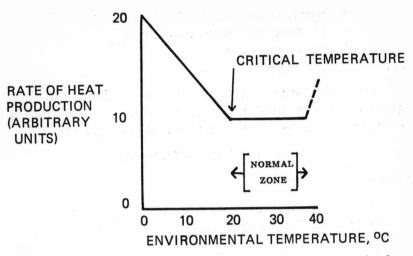

Figure 51. Basal metabolism versus environmental temperature for frogs and rats (from Kleiber [38], p. 163).

BASAL METABOLISM CORRELATIONS

Based on experiments with lambs, it seems to be true that the fetus in the uterus has a basal metabolic rate (per kg of weight) similar to the maternal organism (17). But tissue separated from its host organism is not homeothermic. For example, the metabolic rate of the rat brain is influenced by environmental factors in the same way as poikilothermic bass brain slices (38). In general, the metabolic rate of poikilothermic animals, enzyme systems, and isolated tissue all show a temperature dependence (38).

In 1894, Rubner showed that the amount of heat produced by a dog is equal to the sum of the heats of combustion of the catabolized fat and protein minus the heat of combustion of the urine produced (38). It was later shown that 4.75 kcal of basal heat given off was equivalent to one liter of oxygen consumed (38). The heat loss was also correlated empirically with temperature as (38):

$$M = [9.1 + 2.2\,(T_o - 28)]\,[(T_R - T_S)]$$

where

M = basal heat loss, kcal/m².hr
T_o = environmental temperature, °C
T_R = rectal temperature, °C
T_S = skin temperature, °C

We know that the basal metabolic rate varies from specie to specie, as given by Table XXIII. These data can be correlated for a range of 10^{-2} to 10^4 body weights in kilograms (38, 17):

$$\log M = 1.83 + 0.75 \log W$$

where

M = basal metabolic rate, kcal/day
W = adult body weight, kg

TABLE XXIII

BASAL METABOLISM DATA FOR VARIOUS SPECIES OF ANIMALS*

	Average Weight kg	Basal Metabolism $\dfrac{kcal}{day}$	$\dfrac{kcal}{day.kg}$	$\dfrac{kcal}{day.m^2}$
Horse	441	4990	11.3	948
Cow	300	4221	14.1	
Pig	128	2443	19.1	1078
Man	64.3	2065	32.1	1042
Sheep	46.4	1254	27.1	
Dog	15.2	783	51.5	1039
Rabbit	5.33	233	43.8	
"	4.33	191	44.1	
"	3.57	164	46.0	
"	2.98	167	56.0	
"	2.46	119	48.3	
"	2.3	173	75.1	776
"	1.52	83	54.7	
Rat	0.28	28.1	100.3	
Mouse	0.021	3.6	171.5	

*From Kleiber (38), pages 181, 205

The basal rate for female rats is 248 kcal/day.kg at birth, goes to a maximum of about 300 kcal/day.kg at 3 to 5 days of age and then decreases to approximately 122 kcal/day.kg at 100 days of age. Table XXIV presents these data for rats.

TABLE XXIV

BASAL METABOLISM DATA FOR FEMALE RATS*

Age days	Body Wt. grams	Metabolic Rate		
		$\dfrac{kcal}{day.kg}$	$\dfrac{kcal}{day.kg^{3/4}}$	$\dfrac{kcal}{day.kg^{2/3}}$
0-2	6.5	248	85	47
3-5	9.1	301	98	61
7-10	10	260	84	55
12	14	283	99	67
14-16	27	197	80	58
20	34	206	87	65
30-34	66	216	109	87
40-44	105	203	116	96
50-53	150	159	99	85
75-79	179	134	87	75
100-116	230	114	79	70
202-227	273	104	75	67
300-317	300	102	74	69
401-500	310	100	75	67
601-700	317	104	77	70
801-900	345	113	86	78
901-1000	284	121	89	80

*From Kleiber (38), page 227

For human babies, basal metabolism follows the curve,

$$\log M = \log k + n \log W$$

where

M = basal metabolic rate

W = weight

k,n = constants

Between 0 to 6 hours of age, the basal oxygen consumption of babies is fairly constant (17). Then during the six to 16 hour lifespan, there is a steep rise, reaching a maximum at about one week as shown in Table XXV. The basal rate then remains constant at about 7 ml O_2/min.kg until 18 months of age when it declines with increasing age. Some relationships which are applicable based on the data in Table XXV are:

TABLE XXV

OXYGEN CONSUMPTION AS A FUNCTION OF THE AGE OF NEWBORN HUMAN BABIES*

Age of the Baby	Oxygen Consumption ml O_2/min.kg		
	Reference (17)	Bruck[1]	Benedict and Talbot[2]
0-6 hr	4.76	4.77	5.34
18-30 hr	6.59		5.94
2-4 days	6.70	5.27	6.22
6-10 days	7.02	5.10	6.08

1 ml O_2 consumed is equivalent to 5 calories of heat given off

1 ml O_2/min. consumed is equivalent to 300 calories/hr of heat given off

[1]Temperature Regulation in the newborn infant, Biol. Neonat. *3*, 65-119 (1961).

[2]The physiology of the newborn infant, Carnegie Institute of Washington, Publication No. 233 (1915).

*From Hill and Rahimtulla (17)

babies (below 12 kg weight): basal O_2 consumption, $\dfrac{ml}{min} = 7.2\ W$

babies (above 12 kg weight): basal O_2 consumption, $\dfrac{ml}{min} = 20\ W^{0.6}$

where W is the body weight in kilograms.

There is apparently an increase of oxygen consumption during the early, tenuous hours and days of life as the struggle to establish a life pattern goes on. By the end of the first week the baby becomes homeothermic and the level of basal metabolism and oxygen consumption no longer depends on such factors as rectal temperature (17).

For children, the metabolic rate which starts at about 50 kcal/day.kg at birth, reaches a maximum of about 56 kcal/day.kg and then decreases to about 34 kcal/day.kg at twelve years of age (38). For little girls and women, the variation in basal metabolism is as shown in Figure 52.

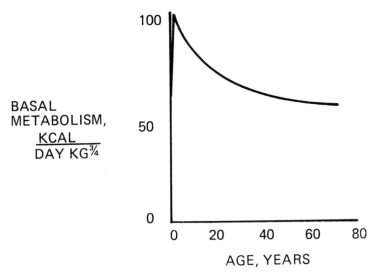

Figure 52.   Change in basal metabolism of female humans as a function of age (from Kleiber [38], p. 224, 228).

Tables XXVI and XXVII summarize some extensive basal metabolism data collected for human males, showing variations with height, weight, body water content and surface area. Figures 53 and 54 show these data graphically, in more readable form.

These data, for men and women, have been connected to age and height as well as body weight, as (38):

TABLE XXVI

BASAL METABOLIC DATA ON HUMAN MALES AS A FUNCTION OF MANY BODY VARIABLES*

Variable	Age Decades							
	20-29	30-39	40-49	50-59	60-69	70-79	80-89	90-99
Height, cm	176.1	171.2	171.9	167.5	166.8	164.0	164.8	162.1
Weight, kg	82.2	71.4	65.8	64.5	65.2	61.1	64.3	58.0
Surface Area, m²	1.97	1.85	1.78	1.72	1.73	1.66	1.70	1.60
Total Body Water (TBW), L	40.95	38.44	35.86	35.15	32.96	31.64	31.13	30.89
Oxygen Consumption, cc/min.	253	218	210	207	196	187	180	163
Oxygen Consumption, cc/min.TBW	6.0	5.7	6.0	5.9	6.0	6.0	5.8	5.2
Basal Heat Production, kcal/hr.	73.52	63.15	60.69	59.73	56.55	54.22	52.01	47.07
Basal Heat Production, kcal/hr.m²	36.83	33.98	34.44	34.43	32.67	32.84	30.64	29.01
Basal Heat Production, kcal/hr.kg	.896	.886	.924	.926	.868	.888	.809	.813

From Shock, et al. (13)

TABLE XXVII

MORE BASAL METABOLIC DATA FOR HUMAN MALES*

Variable	Age Decades						
	20-29	30-39	40-49	50-59	60-69	70-79	80-89
Weight, kg	70.97	77.3	79.01	77.2	79.02	71.42	70.08
Basal O₂ Consumption, cc/min	247.2	247.4	237.4	228.7	228.3	204.4	197.8
Basal Heat, kcal/hr	71.4	71.4	68.5	66.2	66.0	59.2	57.0
Basal Heat, kcal/hr.kg	1.005	.924	.867	.857	.835	.830	.812

*From Norris, Lundy and Shock (18)

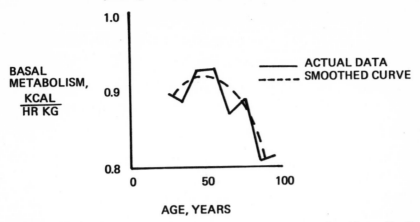

Figure 53.   Basal metabolism versus age for human males (from Shock, et al. [13]).

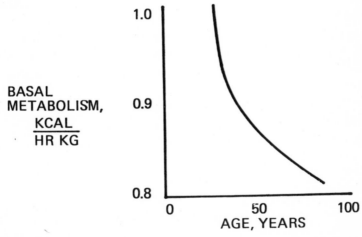

Figure 54.   Basal metabolism versus age for human males (from Norris, Lundy and Shock [18]).

men: $M = 66.47 + 13.75\,W + 5.003H - 6.77A$
women: $M = 655.1 + 0.56W + 1.85H - 4.67A$

where

M = basal metabolic rate, kcal/day
W = body weight, kg

H = height, cm
A = age, years.

Other relationships have been developed (38):

men: $M = 71.2W^{3/4} [1 + 0.004 (30 - A) + 0.010 (H - 43.4)]$
women: $M = 65.8W^{3/4} [1 + 0.004 (30 - A) + 0.018 (H - 42.1)]$

and (17)

men: $M = 70W^{0.75}$

Table XXVI allows for variations with total body water, implying that perhaps this factor is important in basal metabolism determinations. Table XXVIII also shows this variation. When basal metabolism is computed on a total body water basis as shown in Tables XXVI and XXVIII, basal metabolism becomes essentially a constant, not varying with age. This behavior is contrary to the usual decrease in basal metabolism with age, when calculated on a weight or surface area basis. Whether total body water is a significant parameter needs to be more clearly established. Perhaps basal metabolism calculations need to account for the "inert" materials.

There may be more to basal metabolism data than is apparent at first. We can plot these values as a function of age quite readily and note that the curves obtained are monotonically

TABLE XXVIII

BASAL METABOLISM AS A FUNCTION OF AGE AND
TOTAL BODY WATER*

Variable	Age Decades							
	20-29	30-39	40-49	50-59	60-69	70-79	80-89	90-99
Total Body Water (TBW), L	32.6	33.8	40.5	35.0	26.8	29.9	23.7	20.2
Basal Heat, kcal/hr.m²	35.6	33.5	34.6	31.3	31.3	31.3	28.5	30.7
Basal Heat, kcal/hr.TBW	1.85	1.79	1.69	1.65	1.83	1.71	1.80	2.13

*From Baker, Shock and Norris (14)

decreasing (steadily diminishing values). So it becomes possible to speculate on whether these trends continue until death, whether basal metabolism curves can tell us anything about impending death. Is there a critical value for basal metabolism, below which the organism simply cannot function? Does the "idling engine" stall below a certain rate of operation? Figure 55 shows for rats the effect on basal metabolism of extreme starvation leading to death. On the last day (at death), the basal metabolism is about 50 kcal/day.kg$^{3/4}$ at 35°C and 35 kcal/day.kg$^{3/4}$ at 30°C. Is there a critical level of basal metabolism below which death occurs? And is this critical value dependent on temperature? The data of Figure 55 may suggest this but much more information is required before any conclusions can be drawn.

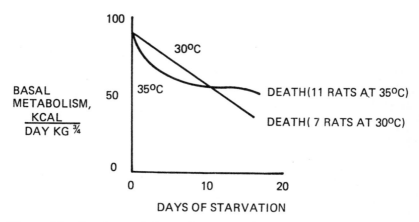

Figure 55. Basal metabolism changes with starvation for rats (from Kleiber [38], p. 241).

ENTROPY, BASAL METABOLISM AND LIFE EXPECTANCY

Homeothermic mammalian species differing greatly in temporal lifespan may have equal caloric (basal metabolism) lifespans. The total heat given off, measured over the lifespan, seems to indicate that animals generate approximately the same amount of heat (33, 59) as shown in Table XXIX. Homo sapiens have about a fourfold greater lifetime accumulation and are exceptions.

TABLE XXIX

BASAL HEAT PRODUCTION OVER THE
LIFETIMES OF SOME ANIMALS*

Specie	Life Expectancy years	Body Temperature °C	Lifetime Energy Production $\dfrac{cal}{kg.°K}$
Rats	4	38.1	5.7 x 10²
Dairy Cattle	30	38.6	5.5 x 10²
Mules	20	38	5.2 x 10²
Horses	20	37.8	4.5 x 10²
Guinea Pigs	7	38	4.2 x 10²
Humans	75	37	21.4 x 10²

*From Hershey (59)

The rate of living probably has a temperature coefficient comparable to that of other biochemical processes. This is seen as support for the hypothesis that aging depletes some sort of living substance that occurs as a consequence of physicochemical activities (32). Imagos of D. subobscura transferred to a temperature of 26°C after four to 24 days at 20°C lived as long as if they had lived their entire imaginal lives at 26°C. This data has led to a theory which hypothesizes that the initial rate of aging is independent of temperature, but longevity decreases with increasing temperature in later life (32).

But there are those who say that the rate of aging is not simply a consequence of metabolic activity, but of the more significant property of entropy production* — and entropy production in highly evolved organisms such as vertebrates is governed by the size and capacity of the overall information and control system (32). Thus we implicitly introduce the concept of a biological clock and attempt to develop the idea that perhaps there is a better way of measuring age, using some inherent, transitory physiologic variable rather than the usual measure of seconds, minutes, hours, etc. Many organic processes (including

---

*Defined as a measure of the randomness or disorder of a system.

entropy production) are found to be run at rates proportional to the reciprocal of temperature.

Some researchers define an organizational entropy, S_{org}, and show that (32):

$$S_{org} = R (\ln \mu - \ln \rho) + \text{constant}$$

where

R   = the gas constant
ρ = the maturation rate for a definitive stage of development of the organism
μ = the mean metabolic rate for the same stage
μ/ρ = a measure of the energy cost of carrying the development of an organism from one defined stage to another.

Figure 56 shows how typical curves for ρ and μ look for drosophila eggs and larva pupae, which leads to curves such as in Figure 57.

Apparently there may be an optimum temperature for life, where entropy generation (S_{org}) is at a minimum, as seen in Figure 57. A displacement on either side of this optimum temperature results in an increase in the organizational entropy. A lower rate of entropy production permits the organism to live longer and do more metabolic work. The rate of aging and

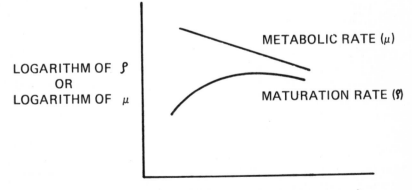

Figure 56.   Logarithmic relationship for maturation rate and metabolic rate versus the reciprocal of temperature (from Sacher [32]).

maturation are related to the rate of entropy production of the whole system (32): aging is related not only to how much metabolic work is performed but to how well the work is done, in entropy terms.

Homo sapiens are the longest-lived mammals. To live even longer, we need to decrease entropy production by minimizing the cost of living in terms of increased information processing and control. Once we have analyzed the requirements, then by improving the genotype by eugenic procedures we can engineer ourselves into longer life (32).

There are other definitions of entropy

$$S = k \log D$$

or

$$S = k \log P$$

where

S = entropy
k = the Boltzmann constant
D = a measure of atomic disorder
P = probability, related to the possibility of having some particular organic structure, or being at a particular state of development.

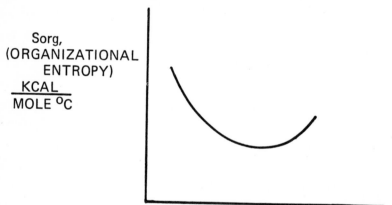

Sorg,
(ORGANIZATIONAL
ENTROPY)
KCAL
MOLE °C

RECIPROCAL OF TEMPERATURE, $\frac{1}{T}$

Figure 57. Organizational entropy versus the reciprocal of temperature (from Sacher [32]).

Maximum entropy content may correspond to death (38). If the death of an organism is viewed as the state characterized by maximum entropy, then we ought to determine the total entropy production during the lifetime of an organism. Comparisons of the total lifetime entropy production for different organisms should be enlightening, and from these figures perhaps some inferences can be made concerning life expectancy. For example, it may be that life continues so long as entropy production is at, or greater than, some minimum level.

But we need some relatively simple way of calculating entropy production for an animal as a whole. By considering the homeothermic animals as isothermal, infinite heat reservoirs, it should be possible to measure the heat given off (basal metabolism), body temperature, body weight, and calculate some measure of entropy production. As a function of the age of the animal, we can establish numbers with units such as $\frac{\text{basal heat/time}}{\text{weight.temperature}}$ or $\frac{\text{calories/hr}}{\text{kg.°K}}$. These are entropy units, so it is possible to define and calculate an "organic entropy" for each organism. By doing these experiments on various species and calculating organic entropy generation over their lifetimes, some of the following questions may be answered.

1. Is there a minimum level of entropy production required for life? Will an organism die when this entropy production drops below this critical level? Does this critical level vary for each specie?

2. Do animals, in their lifetimes, generate predetermined quantities of organic entropy as suggested by the data in Table XXIX? Do all animals in their lifetimes, generate an equal amount of organic entropy?

3. Is man's "higher" form of development indicated by a higher lifetime entropy generation than the "lower" animals as shown in Table XXIX?

4. Should a new age scale be defined, based on organic entropy production?

The answers to these questions await more extensive data.

CHAPTER 9

SUMMING UP

WE HAVE PRESENTED MICROSCOPIC and macroscopic theories of aging. Clearly all the ideas and equations are related; no one theory has the exclusive claim to the truth. We seem to be getting closer to an understanding of the aging process, however, recognizing that the biochemical processes on the subcellular, molecular level are the initiators. And if everything is known, will it be possible to slow down — or halt — the aging process? There is some evidence that we can slow it down, but it is unlikely that we will ever be able to halt the aging process and live forever. For the second law of thermodynamics (56) states that an engine (the organism) cannot be 100 percent efficient. The sketch below illustrates this in a simple way: all the energy coming in cannot be converted to work (living). We know from the second law of thermodynamics that there must be some waste released. So in the course of living, some waste products are produced; and it is these waste products which somehow induce what we call aging.

We can speculate on the meaning of age and how to measure it — based not on years, but on energy or entropy levels. We may not be able to halt the aging process completely, but it should be possible to slow it down so we may live longer and better. Perhaps along the way we may find a more meaningful measure of our biological age.

$$\begin{array}{ccccc} \text{Energy} & & \text{An Engine} & & \\ \text{or} & \rightarrow & \text{or} & \rightarrow & \text{Work} \\ \text{Entropy} & & \text{A Living Organism} & & \\ & & \downarrow & & \\ & & \text{Waste} & & \end{array}$$

GLOSSARY

acentric	Placed off center
amino acid	Organic compounds which are essential parts of the protein molecule
amoeba	A specie of protozoa
anabolic	The metabolic processes by which simple substances are synthesized into the complex materials of living tissue
aneuploidy	Having a chromosome number which is unusual, not a multiple of the haploid set of chromosomes
angstrom	A unit of length equal to one hundred-millionth of a centimeter
arterioles	Small terminal branches of the arteries
arteriosclerosis	A thickening and hardening of arterial walls which interferes with circulation
atherosclerosis	The accumulation of cellular materials in arterial walls
atmosphere	A unit of pressure corresponding to 14.7 pounds per square inch
ATP	Adenosine triphosphate, the chemical which helps provide the energy of life processes
aural	Related to the ear
bacteriophage	A viral organism that infects bacteria
bacterium	A unicellular microrganism
basal metabolism	The rate of heat given off by the body when in a resting condition
binary fission	The asexual reproductive process in which a unicellular organism splits into two equal cells
bone marrow	Soft tissue in the hollow of long bones. Divided into red and yellow marrow, it is active in the production of red blood cells

141

°C	Temperature, degrees Centigrade
catalyst	An agent which causes or accelerates a chemical reaction without itself being consumed by the reaction
cc	Cubic centimeters
cerebellar cortex	The outer layer of the cerebellum of the brain, responsible for regulation of voluntary muscle movement
cerebral cortex	The outer layer of grey tissue of the brain, responsible for some nervous functions
ceroid	A waxy, pigmented material
chelating	A class of chemicals which can bind to metals
chondrocyte	A cartilage cell
chromatin	A complex of nucleic acids and proteins which can be stained with dyes for identification
chromosome	A DNA-containing linear arrangement of cell material responsible for the determination and transmission of hereditary characteristics
cilia	Fine cytoplasmic thread projecting from the surface of the cell, used for propulsion
clones	Identical cells descended from a common ancestor
cm	Centimeter
collagen	The fibrous constituent of bone, cartilage and connective tissue
colloid	A suspension of finely-divided solid particles in a liquid
conjugation	Sexual reproduction of protozoans where they exchange genetic material
creatinuria	An increased concentration of creatine in the urine
cysteine	An amino acid
cytolysis	The dissolution of a cell
cytoplasm	Any part of the cell outside of the nucleus.

It is a thick, viscous, colorless material, essential in the life process

denaturation	A change in the nature or quality of organic chemicals
diploid cell	The usual body (somatic) cell, having a matched pair of chromosomes
DNA	Deoxyribonucleic acid
dyshomeostasis	Faulty homeostasis
elastin	Part of elastic tissue such as tendons, cartilage and connective tissue
electron	A subatomic, negatively charged particle
endocellular	Produced inside the cells
endocrine system	The internal secretions of glands such as the thyroid or adrenal
endogenous	Produced from within the body
endothelial	A squamous form of flat cells which line blood and lymph vessels
enteritis	Inflammation of the intestinal tract
entropy	A measure of the randomness, disorder or chaos in a system, related to its ability to undergo spontaneous change
enzymes	Proteins which function as catalysts in living systems
epidermis	The outer, protective layer of the skin
epithelium	Membrane tissue covering most internal surfaces and organs and the outer surface of the body
erythroblasts	Cells from which red blood cells are derived
ester	Chemicals formed from some acids
eugenic	Human hereditary improvement by genetic control
exocrine	Glandular secretion through ducts, such as saliva
extracellular	Located outside the cells
fascia	The sheet of fibrous tissue beneath the skin surface enveloping the muscles
fats	Organic compounds obtained from animals

	and plants which contain fatty acids. Fatty acids are a group of acids containing carbon, hydrogen and oxygen atoms arranged in a specific configuration
fibril	A small slender fiber
fibroblast	An undifferentiated cell which gives rise to connective tissue
fibrosis	The formation of fibrous tissue
fission	See Binary Fission
flagella	Long filamentous extensions of some cells or unicellular organisms, used for locomotion
free radical	An atom or group of atoms having at least one unpaired electron
gametic	Pertaining to the gametes or germ cells, which are involved in reproduction
ganglia	Nerve cells
gastrocnemius muscle	The large muscle of the legs which allows the foot to be extended and helps to flex the knee
genes	A hereditary unit occupying a fixed location on a chromosome
genome	A completed set of haploid chromosomes (half the number contained in a diploid cell)
genotype	The genetic constitution of an organism
germ cells	Cells involved in reproduction
gingiva	The gums in the mouth which hold the teeth
glial cell	A fibrous supporting cell such as those in the brain which support the neurons
globulin	A class of proteins found in blood, milk and muscle
glomeruli	The plural of glomerulus
glomular	Pertaining to the glomeruli or capillaries of the kidney
glomus	A shunt or by-pass which can regulate blood flow, temperature and conservation of heat

in the region near the skin

Golgi apparatus A network of fibrils, granules and membrane material believed involved in the formation of secretions in the cells

gonad-pituitary Sex, growth and metabolism functions

half-life Half the material is gone

haploid cells Cells having a single set of chromosomes such as the gamete cells

hematoma A localized swelling filled with blood

hematopoietic Having to do with the production of blood by bone marrow, spleen and lymph glands

hepatectomy Excision of a portion of the liver

hepatic Referring to the liver

homeostasis A state of physiologic equilibrium in function and chemistry

homeotherm Animals which maintain a constant body temperature under normal living conditions

hr Hour

hydroxyl The OH grouping, where O is oxygen and H is hydrogen

hypertension Abnormally high blood pressure in the artery

hypoxia Deficiency in the amount of oxygen reaching the tissues

inclusion An abnormal structure (solid or liquid) in the cell nucleus

intracellular Within the cell

intraperitoneally Within the membrane lining of the walls of the abdominal cavity

invagination The deformation of the cell membrane to form a cavity

invertebrate Having no backbone or spinal column

in vitro In laboratory equipment, outside of the body

in vivo In the living body

islets of the pancreas "Islands of Langerhans" which produce insulin

°K	Temperature, degrees Kelvin
karyotype	The number of chromosomes
kcal	Kilocalories (1000 calories)
keratin	A tough, fibrous protein containing sulfur and forming the outer layer of epidermal structures such as hair, nails, horns and hoofs
kg	Kilogram (1000 grams)
L	Liter
labile	Unstable
lactobacillus	Bacteria that convert carbohydrates to lactic acid
leucocyte	The white blood cell, formed in bone marrow and the spleen
ligated	To tie up or constrict
lipids	Fatty substances which together with carbohydrates and proteins constitute the principal structural material of living cells
lipofuscin	Brown pigmented lipid-containing granules found in old tissue
lipoprotein	A protein combined with a lipid group
ln	Natural logarithm
log	Logarithm
lymphocytes	White blood cells formed in lymph nodes and spleen associated with the control of foreign organisms
lysosomes	Membrane-enclosed sacs of digestive enzymes which, when ruptured, lead to the breakdown of the foods or foreign substances in the cell
m^2	Square meters of surface area
macromolecule	A polymer usually composed of 100 or more repeated units
menarche	The first occurrence of menstruation
mercaptan	A sulfur-containing organic compound, where organic means carbon-containing
mesodermal	The intermediate layer of cells, from which

	develop connective tissue, muscles and the vascular systems
metabolic rate	The physical and chemical processes involved in the maintenance of life
microliter	One-millionth of a liter
micromole	One-millionth of a mole
micron	A unit of length equal to one-millionth of a meter
microrganism	A microscopic animal, especially a bacterium or a protozoan
microsome	A cell particle containing RNA which is involved in protein synthesis
milligram	One-thousandth of a gram
milliliter	One-thousandth of a liter
millimole	One-thousandth of a mole
min	Minute
mitochondria	Small granules or rod-shaped structures found in the cell, involved in ATP production (the "powerhouse" of the cell)
mitosis	The sequence of cell division in which each new cell contains the requisite number of chromosomes
mixoploid cells	Those cells which have different numbers of genomes in its cell population
ml	Milliliter
mole	An amount of material equal to its molecular weight
mollusk	Marine invertebrate, including edible shellfish
morphogenic	Causing the evolutionary changes
morphological	Pertaining to form and structure
mucopolysaccharide	Chemicals which form sticky or lubricating fluids of the body
mucosa	A mucus membrane, containing mucosal cells
mucosal cells	Cells which secrete mucus

muscular dystrophy Gradual but irreversible muscular deterioration

myeloblast Bone marrow cell which develops into intermediate cells from which finally are derived the leucocytes

myocardial infarction By a loss of blood supply, the heart muscle is damaged or the tissue dies

myocardium The muscle tissue of the heart

neoplasm An abnormal growth of tissue, such as a tumor

nephritis Inflammation of the kidney

nephron One of the tubes for excretion in the kidney

neurons Nerve cells

nitrogenous Containing nitrogen

nuclei The spherical material within living cells that contains the hereditary material and controls its metabolism, growth and reproduction

nucleic acid Polymers built up from nucleotides (which are composed of sugars, phosphate groups and organic materials). RNA and DNA are composed of nucleic acids

nucleoside A chemical made from a sugar and a derivative of a nucleic acid

organelles Specialized parts of a cell, analogous to the internal organs of multicellular animals

organic Associated with living organisms, usually containing carbon and hydrogen atoms

organic-selenium complex Combinations of selenium and organic materials

osmotic Pertaining to osmosis, the diffusion of fluids through the cell membrane until pressure inside and outside are equal

ova Female reproduction cells of animals

ovacytes Egg cells of the ovary

papilla Small nipplelike projections which produce the sense of taste

parenchymal cells	Cells of organ tissue as distinguished from connective tissue cells
peroxidation	A chemical reaction which yields peroxides
peroxide	A substance which contains an excess of oxygen such as hydrogen peroxide
poikilotherms	Living things which assume a body temperature of the environment
plaque	A small disk-shaped formation or growth
polymerization	The uniting of two or more chemical units
polysaccharide	A combination of nine or more units of starch or cellulose molecules
polyunsaturated	Pertaining to long-chain compounds, especially fats, with many double bonds such as $C=C$ where C is the carbon atom. These are generally the softer, sometimes liquid fats
primordial	A cell of an organism in the earliest stage of development
proteinase	An enzyme which can break down protein
protoplasm	The jelly-like material inside the cells, essential to life function
protozoa	Single-celled, microscopic animals
pseudopod	A protoplasmic extension generated by protozoa for purposes of locomotion and contacting food
pulmonary artery	The artery in which blood travels directly from the heart to the lungs
Purkinje cell	A type of brain cell which can integrate information received from many neurons
pyknosis	A degenerative condition of a cell nucleus, marked by clumping of the chromosomes and shrinking of the nucleus
rad	A unit of energy absorbed from radiation
renal	Pertaining to the kidney
reticular	Resembling a net structure
reticuloendothelial	Related to the liver, spleen, lymph nodes,

system	bone marrow, involved in antibody formation in combating infections
reticulum	The net-like membrane formation
RNA	Ribonucleic acid
roentgen	An obsolete unit of radiation dosage
rotifer	A small, multicellular aquatic organism
saturated	Pertaining to long-chain compounds, especially fats, with few double bonds such as $C = C$ where C is the carbon atom. These are generally the hard, usually solid, fats
sebum	The oily secretion of sebaceous glands, lubricating the epidermis and oiling the hair
serum	The clear yellowish fluid obtained when whole blood is filtered and the solid components are removed
smooth muscle	The involuntary muscle of internal organs such as the bladder and blood vessels, excluding the heart
somatic cell	Any bodily cell other than a reproductive cell
specific gravity	Weight of an object compared to the weight of the same volume of water
spermatocytes	Cells which give rise to spermatozoa
spermatozoa	Mature, male germ cells—the specific output of the testes
spermatozonia	The sperm cell
squamous cells	A single layer of cells, such as those which cover exposed surfaces of the body
stem cells	Those cells which support or connect organs
stochastic	Random or statistical
subcutaneous	Located just beneath the skin
taste buds	Spherical nests of cells responsible for the sense of taste
thalamus	Part of the brain which relays sensory stimuli to the cerebral cortex
unsaturated	Pertaining to compounds that share more than one chemical bond, represented as

	$C=C$, where C is the carbon atom and $=$ represents the unsaturated bond
uretha	The canal through which urine is discharged
vacuole	Membrane-bounded chamber in a cell
vacuolization	The generation of small cavities (vacuoles) in the protoplasm of the cell
vertebrate	Organisms having a backbone or spinal column, such as birds and mammals
viral	Of, pertaining to, or caused by a virus
yr	Year
zygotic	Related to the zygote which is the cell formed by the union of two gametes

REFERENCES

1. Selye, H.: Is aging curable? *Science Digest, 46*:1, 1959.
2. Frisch, R. E., and Revelle, R.: Height and weight at menarche and a hypothesis of critical body weights and adolescent events. *Science, 169*:379, 1970.
3. Hayflick, L.: The limited in vitro lifetime of human diploid cell strains. *Experimental Cell Research, 27*:614, 1965.
4. Harman, D.: Free radical theory of aging: Effect of free radical inhibitors on the lifespan of male LAF mice — second experiment. *The Gerontologist, 8*:13, 1968.
5. Harman, D.: Role of serum copper in coronary atherosclerosis. *Circulation, 28*:658, 1963.
6. Curtis, H. H., Czernik, C., and Tilley, J.: Tumor induction as a measure of genetic damage and repair in somatic cells in mice. *Radiation Research, 34*:315, 1968.
7. Harman, D.: Prolongation of the normal lifespan and inhibition of spontaneous cancer by antioxidants. *Journal of Gerontology, 16*:247, 1961.
8. Harman, D.: The free radical theory of aging: The effect of age on serum mercaptan levels. *Journal of Gerontology, 15*:38, 1960.
9. Curtis, H. J.: Recovery of mammals from late radiation effects. *Radiation and Aging*, Lindop, P. J., and Sacher, G. A. (Ed.), Taylor & Francis, London, p. 105, 1966.
10. Comfort, A.: Longevity and mortality in dogs of four breeds, *Journal of Gerontology, 15*:126, 1960.
11. Comfort, A.: Nutrition and longevity in animals. *Proceedings of the Nutritional Society, 19*:125, 1960.
12. Comfort, A.: The duration of life in mollusks. *Proceedings of the Malacological Society of London, 32*:219, 1957.
13. Shock, N. W., Watkin, D. M., Yiengst, M. J., Norris, A. H., Gaffney, G. W., Gregerman. R. I. and Falzone, J. A.: Age differences in the water content of the body related to basal oxygen consumption in males. *Journal of Gerontology, 18*:1, 1963.
14. Baker, S. P., Shock, N. W., and Norris, A. H.: Influence of age and obesity in women on basal oxygen consumption expressed in terms of total water and intracellular water. In Shock, N. (Ed.): *Biological Aspects of Aging.* New York, Columbia University Press, p. 84, 1962.
15. Pope, F., Lunsford, W., and McCay, C. M.: Experimental prolongation of the life span. *The Neurologic and Psychiatric Aspects of the*

Disorders of Aging. Proceedings of the Association for Research in Nervous and Mental Disease. Baltimore, Williams and Williams, vol. XXXV, p. 61, 1956.

16. McCay, C. M., Pope, F., and Lunsford, W.: Experimental prolongation of the life span. *Bulletin of the New York Academy of Medicine,* 32:91, 1956.
17. Hill, J. R., and Rahimtulla, K. A.: Heat balance and the metabolic rate of newborn babies in relation to environmental temperature; and the effect of age and weight on basal metabolic rate. *Journal of Physiology, 180:*239, 1965.
18. Norris, A. H., Lundy, T., and Shock, N. W.: Trends in selected indices of body compositions in men between the ages 30 and 80 years. *Annals of the New York Academy of Science, 110:*623, 1963.
19. Epstein, M. H., and Thorne, P. R.: Respiration of isolated cerebellar neurons using an automatic fiber optic cartesian diver. *Experimental Neurology, 26:*586, 1970.
20. Leake, C. D.: Biological mechanism in aging. *Geriatrics 19:*229, 1964.
21. Comfort, A.: Feasibility in age research. *Nature (London), 217:*320, 1968.
22. Comfort, A.: Mortality and the nature of age processes. *The Journal of the Institute of Actuaries, 84:*263, 1958.
23. Comfort, A.: The biology of aging. In Rook, A., and Champion, R. H. (Eds.): *Progress in the Biological Sciences in Relation to Dermatology.* London, Cambridge University Press, p. 55, 1960.
24. Hayflick, L.: Senescence and cultured cells. In Shock, N. (Ed.): *Perspective in Experimental Gerontology.* Thomas, Springfield, p. 195, 1966.
25. Pope, F., Lunsford, W., and McCay, C. M.: Experimental prolongation of the lifespan. *Journal of Chronic Diseases, 4:*153, 1956.
26. Hainsworth, F. R., and Wolf, L. L.: Regulation of oxygen consumption and body temperature during torpor in a hummingbird. *Science, 168:*369, 1970.
27. Comfort, A.: Physiology, homeostasis and aging. *Gerontologia, 14:*224, 1968.
28. Hayflick, L.: Human cells and aging. *Scientific American. 218:*32, 1968.
29. Huennekens, F. M.: In vitro aging of erythrocytes. In Strehler, B. L. (Ed.): *The Biology of Aging.* American Institute of Biological Sciences, Baltimore, Waverly, p. 200, 1960.
30. Mildvan, S., and Strehler, B. L.: A critique of theories of mortality. In, Strehler, B. L. (Ed.) *The Biology of Aging.* American Institute of Biological Sciences, Baltimore, Waverly, p. 216, 1960.
31. Curtis, H. J.: Biological mechanisms underlying the aging process. *Science, 141:*686, 1963.
32. Sacher, G. A.: The complementarity of entropy terms for the temper-

ature-dependence of development and aging. *Annals of the New York Academy of Science, 138*:680, 1967.

33. Kohn, R. R.: *Principles of Mammalian Aging.* Englewood Cliffs, Prentice-Hall, 1971.
34. Milne, L. J., and Milne, M.: *The Ages of Life,* New York, Harcourt, Brace and World, 1968.
35. Bakerman, S. (Ed.): *Aging Life Processes.* Springfield, Thomas, 1969.
36. Brues, A. M. and Sacher, G. A.: *Aging and Levels of Biological Organization.* Chicago, University of Chicago Press, 1965.
37. Lwoff, A.: *Biological Order.* Cambridge, M.I.T., 1962.
38. Kleiber, M.: *The Fire of Life.* New York, Wiley, 1961.
39. Evans, W. E. D.: *The Chemistry of Death.* Springfield, Thomas, 1963.
40. Birren, J. E. (Ed.): *Handbook of Aging and the Individual.* Chicago, University of Chicago Press, 1959.
41. Verzar, F.: *Lectures on Experimental Gerontology.* Springfield, Thomas, 1963.
42. Strehler, B. L.: *Time, Cells and Aging.* New York, Academic, 1962.
43. Bjorksten, J.: A match for Methuselah. *The Cincinnati Enquirer Sunday Magazine,* Cincinnati, p. 8, Feb. 20, 1972.
44. Leighton, F. S.: Unlocking the secrets of aging. *The Cincinnati Enquirer Sunday Magazine,* Cincinnati, p. 47, Nov. 9, 1969.
45. Pryor, W. A.: Free radical pathology. *Chemical and Engineering News,* p. 34, June 7, 1971.
46. Harman, D.: Role of free radicals in mutation, cancer, aging and the maintenance of life. *Radiation Research, 16*:753, 1962.
47. Harman, D.: Free radical theory of aging: Effect of free radical reaction inhibitors on the mortality rate of male LAF mice. *Journal of Gerontology, 23*:476, 1968.
48. Passwater, R. A., and Welker, P. A.: Human aging research, part two. *American Laboratory,* p. 21, May, 1971.
49. Passwater, R. A., and Welker, P. A.: Human aging research, part one. *American Laboratory,* p. 36, April, 1971.
50. Hart, J. W., and Carpenter, D.: Toward an integrated theory of aging. *American Laboratory,* p. 31, April, 1971.
51. Sanadi, D. R.: Letter to the editor. *Chemical and Engineering News,* p. 9, May 10, 1971.
52. Andleman, R. C.: Letter to the editor. *Chemical and Engineering News,* p. 9, May 10, 1971.
53. Curtis, H. J.: A composite theory of aging. *The Gerontologist, 6*:143, 1966.
54. Comfort, A.: Mutation, autoimmunity and aging. *Lancet, 2*:138, 1963.
55. Carpenter, D. G.: Biological aging as a diffusion phenomenon. *Bulletin of Mathematical Physics, 31*:487, 1969.

56. Lee, J. F., and Sears, F. W.: Thermodynamics. Cambridge, Addison-Wesley, 1955.
57. Brody, S.: *Bioenergetics and Growth*. New York, Van Nostrand Reinhold, 1945.
58. Burton, D. R., and Collier, L.: The development of water conditioned suits. *Royal Aircraft Establishment Technical Note, No. Mech. Eng. 400*, London Ministry of Aviation, 1964. (Unpublished contribution of Dr. McK. Kerslake, Royal Air Force Institute of Aviation.)
59. Hershey, D.: Entropy, basal metabolism and life expectancy. *Gerontologia*, 7:245, 1963.

INDEX

A

Accident frequency for coal miners, 29
Aging population 65 years or older, 27
Antioxidants, 87-97
Aorta strength, 36
Athletes and aging, 32-33
Autoimmunity, 74-75, 78, 104-112

B

Basal Metabolic rate, 37, 115-117, 123-140
Blood pressure, 37
Body temperature, 123-140
Body weight and lifespan, 20, 22
Brain size with age, 25
Brain weight and lifespan, 21-22, 54-55, 60-62
Breathing capacity with age, 35, 117
Brody-Failla theory, 118-119, 121

C

Calcium levels with age, 44
Cancer, 63-64
Cardiac output with age, 35, 37
Cell growth, 49-52
Cell regeneration, 62-64
Cell senescence, 53-62, 65
Chemical aging, 73
Chromosomes, 46, 55, 58, 108
Collagen aging, 31, 42-45, 73, 75, 98-104, 120-122
Critical temperatures, 125-127
Cross-linking (see Collagen aging)

D

Diet and lifespan, 23-24, 77-78, 90-97, 113-114
Differentiating cells, 47
Diffusion Theory, 120-122
Distensibility of skin, 43
DNA, 46, 92, 99-100, 104, 106
Driving a car, 40

E

Edison's productivity with age, 33
Elastic fibers, 44
Endocrine system, 39, 105
Entropy, 65, 115, 135-140
Exercise and lifespan, 69
Extracellular aging, 73

F

Free radicals, 75, 79, 81-98

G

Genes, 46
Gompertz survival equation, 116-120

H

Heartbeats and lifespan, 22-23
Homeotherms, 125

I

Illumination requirements, 40-41
Information theory, 64

K

Killing stresses, 120

L

Labile cells, 49
Leading causes of death, 66-67
Life expectancy, 5, 26, 27, 96, 135
Lifespan of mammals, fish and invertebrates, 8-12
Lifespan of trees, 10-11
Lipid peroxidation, 81-98
Lipofuscin, 56, 74, 94, 122
Long-lived fixed post-mitotic cells, 48
Loss of strength, 28-31, 36, 38

M

Memory loss, 38
Mongolism, 58
Mucopolysaccharides, 44

157

N

Near point of the eye, 42
Nerve conduction velocity, 37-38

O

Old age pigments, 56
Oxygen effect on lifespan, 15, 57, 85-87, 89-90, 115-117, 125-126, 130-132
Ozone and lifespan, 89-90

P

Permanent cells, 49
Poikilotherms, 125
Predicting final height, 24
Promine, 53
Pupil diameter in the aged, 41

R

Radiation effect on lifespan, 15-20, 75-76, 83-84, 106-110
Rate of living, 113-117, 136
Red blood cells, 58-60
Respiration changes with age, 37
Reticular fibers, 44
Retine, 53
Reverting post-mitotic cells, 47
RNA, 46, 104, 106
Rotifers lifespan, 6, 7

S

Sacher theory, 119, 121
Scientists productivity with age, 34
Second law of thermodynamics, 140

Selenium, 96-97
Serum copper levels, 85
Serum mercaptan levels, 90, 94
Short-lived post-mitotic cells, 47
Simm-Jones theory, 118, 121
Skin temperature, 123-124
Smell, 42
Somatic mutation, 77, 80, 104-112
Stable cells, 49
Stomach acid secretion with age, 36
Strehler-Mildvan theory, 119-121
Survival curves, 5, 8, 68, 95, 110

T

Taste, 40
Taste buds loss, 40
Temperature effect on lifespan, 13-14, 29, 135, 137-138
Tissue transplants, 59

U

Urinary changes, 38

V

Vegetative cells, 47
Vibrations, 42
Vitality, 118-119, 121
Vitamin C, 94, 97, 101
Vitamin E, 87-89, 103

W

Wear and tear, 113-117
Work at elevated temperatures, 29
Writers productivity with age, 34